From Turnover to Teamwork

A RESTAURANTS & INSTITUTIONS BOOK

From Turnover to Teamwork

How to Build and Retain a Customer-Oriented Foodservice Staff

Bill Marvin
The Restaurant Doctor™

John Wiley & Sons, Inc.
New York / Chichester / Brisbane /
Toronto / Singapore

Library of Congress Cataloging in Publication Data:
Marvin, Bill.
    From turnover to teamwork: how to build and retain a customer-
oriented foodservice staff / by Bill Marvin.
        p.   cm.
    Includes index.
    ISBN 0-471-59077-0
    1. Food service—Personnel management—Handbooks, manuals, etc.
    2. Labor turnover—Handbooks, manuals, etc.   I. Title.
    TX911.3.P4M383   1994
    647.95'068'3—dc20   94-4926

Printed in the United States of America

10 9 8 7 6 5 4 3 2 1

Contents

Preface

This book is about how to create a working environment that will encourage your best people to remain with your organization, work together easily, and deliver exceptional service to your guests. The advantage of such an environment is that the same climate that causes your staff to want to stay will also make your guests want to come back more often.

One of my former teachers once commented that life seems to be a series of things to handle. That observation is certainly true of foodservice. In fact, there are so many things to handle that it is easy for managers to become overwhelmed. Putting in more hours is not the answer. If you are not getting the results you want, it is certainly not for lack of effort. Hospitality managers are no doubt among the hardest-working people on the planet! If hard work alone solved problems or made money, we would all be incredibly relaxed, spectacularly successful, and unspeakably rich.

So what happened? Why are so many operators working harder and daily facing more problems, not the least of which is trying to keep the sort of staff needed to deliver a memorable dining experience to their guests? This book will offer some insights into what influences staff retention rates in foodservice or, for that matter, in any business enterprise.

TURNOVER IS NOT THE PROBLEM

Turnover is just a symptom. The underlying causes of turnover in your operation are probably not what you think they are. If you knew the real cause of the problem, you would already be on top of it. Don't think you are alone in this predicament; we all have blind spots.

The real reasons your good people leave can probably be traced to one of your blind spots. This book will shine some light into a few dark corners. It will help you understand why the things that are working well are happening that way. This means that if they get off track, you will be better able to bring them back into line. You may also start to understand why some things are not working, despite your best efforts.

Most of this book is based on my own experiences in "the real world." When I managed the foodservice department of the U.S. Olympic Training Center in Colorado Springs, these approaches cut turnover from 300 percent to 25 percent in six months, increased staff productivity, and doubled athlete patronage. Operators who have applied these principles to a variety of hospitality formats report similar results. This is common-sense material that I regularly present in management seminars across North America.

COMPUTING THE COST OF TURNOVER

The cost of turnover has direct and indirect components. The direct costs are those expenses that arise solely because a worker quits or is terminated. They can be calculated on a per-person basis. Indirect costs arise as a result of the impact that the staff change has on the ongoing operation. They are harder to quantify because they show up as increased costs for the entire operation.

The following summaries should help you put the costs of turnover into perspective. The expense categories in brackets are from *The Uniform System of Accounts for Restaurants* prepared by the National Restaurant Association.

Direct Costs:

Recruiting costs
[Administrative & General Expense]:
    newspaper ads, materials $50– 100

Staff time (present staff)
[Payroll Expense/Employee Benefits]:
    during interviews, orientation, training,
    counselling (20–80 hr × $8) plus 20%
    benefits   200– 800
    administrative paperwork, signing out old
    workers, signing in new workers
    (1–3 hr × $8) plus 20% benefits   10–   30
Staff time (new staff)
[Payroll Expense/Employee Benefits]:
    during orientation, training, counselling
    (10–60 hr × $5) plus 20% benefits   60– 360
Unemployment claims of departed workers
[Employee Benefits]:
    increase in premiums   100– 200
Administration fees for benefits sign-up
[Employee Benefits]   30–   50
Overtime [Payroll Expense/Employee Benefits]:
    allowance for additional hours to cover while
    the position is vacant (30–60 hr × $7.50)
    plus 20% benefits   270– 540
Other turnover-related costs
[Direct Operating Expense]:
    training materials, uniforms, uniform
    cleaning/renovation   200– 400
Direct Cost per Person $930–2,380

Indirect Costs

1. Increased turnover creates inconsistent (decreased) guest service, which tends to lower your reputation in the market, which increases negative word-of-mouth and reduces repeat patronage, resulting in lower sales. *Estimated impact: sales are 5–15% lower.*

2. Increased turnover means more workers with less training, which increases waste and translates into increased product

and operating costs. ***Estimated impact: operating expenses are 5–15% higher.***

3. Increased turnover means the operation is staffed with generally less-productive workers, which contributes to a higher labor cost. ***Estimated impact: labor cost is 10–20% higher.***

4. Increased turnover leads to the loss of team cohesiveness, which increases staff alienation which fuels staff turnover and keeps the process going! ***Estimated impact on sales and operating costs: escalation of the relationships previously outlined.***

In contrast, organizations with lower turnover can expect improvement in all categories (higher sales, lower costs) by approximately the same percentages.

To put the indirect costs into perspective, let's look at their potential impact on a full-service restaurant doing $1 million in annual sales volume. According to the latest *Restaurant Industry Operations Report*, sponsored by the National Restaurant Association, the typical operation has a turnover rate of 95% a year and would have the following operating results:

	Median Operating Results	
	Amount	Ratio
Sales	$1,000,000	100.0%
Cost of Sales	332,000	33.2%
Payroll Expense	294,000	29.4%
Employee Benefits	45,000	4.5%
Other Operating Expenses	171,000	17.1%
Operating Income	158,000	15.8%

Using the relationship discussed above, I projected the impact on the typical operation of a turnover rate 50% higher than the median (150% a year) and 50% lower than the median. The figures which follow reflect that turnover would have the following effect on the sales and operating expenses of the operation:

Category	Impact	Change to Median Figures
Sales	±$100,000	±10% of sales volume
Cost of Sales	±3.3%	±10% of cost of goods
Payroll Expense	±4.4%	±15% of payroll expense
Staff Benefits		same relationship to payroll expense
Other Operating Expenses	+1.7%	+10% of other operating costs (high turnover)
Other Operating Expenses	−0.9%	−5% of other operating costs (low turnover)

Applying the percentage changes to the median percentage figures (e.g., 17.1% + 10% = 18.8%, 17.1% − 5% = 16.2%) produced some revealing results. Interestingly, the difference in operating ratios correlates closely with the higher and lower quartile from the latest *Restaurant Industry Operations Report.*

	With Higher Turnover		With Lower Turnover	
	Amount	Ratio	Amount	Ratio
Sales	900,000	100.0%	1,100,000	100.0%
Cost of Sales	328,700	36.5%	330,000	30.0%
Payroll	304,200	33.8%	275,000	25.0%
Staff Benefits	46,500	5.2%	42,100	3.8%
Other Operating Expenses	169,200	18.8%	178,200	16.2%
Operating Income	51,400	5.7%	274,700	24.9%

This example suggest that higher turnover yielded operating income of more than $100,000 less than the median figures while lower turnover improved the profitability of the median operation by more than $120,000. The difference between high turnover and low turnover could be more than $220,000 a year in lost profits!

Foodservice is hard enough without giving away profits unnecessarily. If you would like to find out how to recover some of this "lost" money, read on!

Gig Harbor, Washington   BILL R. MARVIN
August 1994   THE RESTAURANT DOCTOR™

Acknowledgments

In this section of a book, the author usually lists a bunch of people you don't know and thanks them for contributions you don't understand! It may be a way to repay social and professional obligations or perhaps it's just tradition. I have always wondered whether acknowledgments were of any real value to the reader. Still, I think it important to recognize that this book, or any book, represents far more than one person's notions. In this spirit (and in no special order), I want to thank a few people whose support and ideas contributed to the work you hold in your hands:

Margene Marvin, my wife and good friend
Syd Banks and George Pransky, for helping me understand
Robert Kausen, Life Education
Don Smith, Washington State University
Mike Hurst, 15th Street Fisheries
Linda Beethe, Benefit & Personnel Resources
Bro. Herman Zaccarelli, King's College
Claire Thompson, John Wiley & Sons, Inc.
Mike Bartlett, Restaurants & Institutions
Pat Raleigh and Craig Showalter, HIRE Midwest
Bill Main, The Shore Bird
Chuck Webber, Midwest Foodservice News
Ken Burley, teacher/provocateur
Mike Nemeth, Nemeth's El Tejon
Doyle Paden, Sonic Drive-Ins

Hap Gray, Watermark Restaurants
Sandy Spivey, Taco Bell
Michael Brandson, McGuffey's Restaurants
Tom Lavaris and Su Pinney, Schwartz Bros. Restaurants/Cucina! Cucina!
Randy Rayburn, Sunset Grill
Jim Moffa, Food for Thought
Skip Sack, Applebee's
Frank Henderson and Randy Thurman, Azteca Mexican Restaurants
Rich Boyle, Burger King

Categorically, I am indebted to the members of my former staff at the Olympic Training Center, my colleagues from CHART, the staff members and managers who have attended my seminars in the United States and Canada, and my consulting clients around the country, all of whom have taught me far more than they suspect. I apologize to those whose names should be listed and are missing. Any omission only reflects that I have absorbed your ideas so completely that it is difficult to separate them from my own. My humble thanks to you all.

From Turnover to Teamwork

Part One
Ponder the Problem

Chapter One

Understand Why Workers Leave

The conventional definition of management is getting work done through people, but real management is developing people through work.

> —H.H. Abedi, President,
> Bank of Credit and Commerce, Luxembourg

All turnover is a management problem, either because management failed to provide a productive working environment or because the wrong person was hired in the first place. Don't blame the workers; all they did was ask for a job. It was management that gave it to them. The simple truth is that your staff leaves because they did not want to stay, mainly because they are not getting what they want from the job.

WHAT DO WORKERS WANT?

If the way to improve staff retention is to give your workers what they want, then the obvious question becomes what is your staff looking for? When I ask the question of managers in my seminars, the typical consensus is that the primary concerns of foodservice employees are pay, benefits, and job security. However, when you ask workers the same questions, you get entirely different answers.

Long-time industry educator Brother Herman Zaccarelli quotes a survey in which foodservice workers say that the three main things they want from their jobs are the following:

1. Appreciation for the work that they do
2. Being "in" on things
3. Help with their personal problems

Higher wages, while a factor, placed fifth on the list. It is no wonder that we have trouble keeping people—we don't even know what they want! As this book unfolds, you will see how to structure your operation to provide more of those things your staff wants while improving your productivity and guest service at the same time. For now, just take a hard look at the management style in your establishment and see if it really delivers the top three things your staff wants.

HOW MUCH OF A MOTIVATOR IS MONEY?

Survey results indicate that salary, benefits, and job security are less important to most workers than appreciation and involvement. While pay should be at or above the going rate in your market for positions of similar skill and authority, high wages alone will not be enough to keep good workers if the working conditions and quality of supervision is substandard.

A number of psychologists suggest that money is actually a *de*motivator—that is to say that too little money creates problems, but after a worker's basic financial needs are met, the importance of money to their job satisfaction decreases.

Many managers might be surprised to learn that increased pay can actually *cause* turnover if it is perceived as an attempt to buy the employee's goodwill or atone for continual abuse. In the long run, money cannot make up for neglect, lack of compassion, or poor working conditions. Treating people well is a human equation, with both sides benefiting; it is not a giveaway program. Your staff knows what sort of compensation is appropriate. Beware of giving rewards that are too little, too late.

HOW DO WORKERS FEEL ABOUT WHAT THEY ARE GETTING NOW?

Do you know how *your* staff members really feel about their jobs? It probably won't surprise you to know that the general level of discontent among foodservice workers is high. In the late 1980s and early 1990s, a series of national surveys[1] measured the satisfaction level of hospitality industry workers concerning such things as pay, rewards, organization, working conditions, opportunity for advancement, training, and supervision. The conclusion drawn from these surveys was that most hospitality employees want out.

Among other things, the studies found the following about the attitude of industry workers:

- Part-time and seasonal workers were less satisfied than full-timers. Those working over 40 hours have the highest level of satisfaction. Those over age 36 were the most satisfied full-time workers. Workers over age 61 were the most satisfied part-timers.

- Tipped employees, despite being the highest-compensated hourly workers, were less satisfied with pay than were non-tipped workers. Females were less satisfied than males. High school graduates and vocational workers were happier than those who had attended college. African-Americans and Hispanics were less satisfied than whites, particularly with opportunities for promotion. Teenagers were the least satisfied of all age groups surveyed.

- Except for chefs, workers were generally dissatisfied with pay

[1]The surveys were conducted by Hire Midwest© of Stillwater, MN, and sponsored by Foodservice News of St. Paul, MN, and Opportunities in Hospitality Publications in Moreno Valley, CA.

and rewards. Employees receiving pay raises in the last year of employment were no more satisfied than employees receiving no raises either because the raises were too small or because they were not tied to performance.

- Most workers highly valued advancement but they thought supervisors played favorites when it came to promotions.

- The majority of employees surveyed did not perceive their trainers as competent. Satisfaction with supervision was low and management was criticized for emphasizing the technical rather than the human side of the work. Supervisors often had no experience in the jobs being supervised. In many cases, there was no supervision whatsoever.

- Workers felt that schedules only favored management and that favoritism rather than performance dictated how scheduled hours were awarded. Flex-time scheduling was only valued by full-time students and elderly workers.

With the possible exception of large or multi-unit operators, our industry has just not devoted much thought or energy to the development and effective utilization of human resources. As a result, we have earned a reputation for being a terrible place to work. The popular conception is that people work in foodservice when they cannot find work anywhere else and then only until they can get a "real job." Unless we get our act together, we will be in serious trouble. As an industry, we will tend to attract sufficient workers only when the economy contracts and other employment options are not available. Once business conditions turn around, many of the industry's employees who were formerly displaced from other industries will depart for jobs with higher pay and better working conditions.

WHY DO WORKERS LEAVE?

You can certainly conduct your own surveys to find out what your staff thinks about working for you (and if you think everything is wonderful, perhaps a survey would be enlightening). However, the odds are that the reasons for any staff discontent will be found on the following list. The purpose of this book is to shift your thinking, increase your understanding, and give you some practical tools to correct or eliminate these operational shortcomings. If you want to dedicate time and money to improve your operation, direct it toward the following areas:

- **Lack of recognition or reward** The number one thing that workers want is appreciation for the work that they do. When it is not forthcoming or when exemplary performance is not rewarded, it takes the heart out of conscientious workers.

- **Lack of teamwork** Super stars or individuals who are only interested in advancing their own agenda are just as damaging to effective teamwork as are workers with lesser skills who insist on going it alone. This sort of selfishness will kill the initiative of team players and drive them away because they know that exemplary guest service is a team sport.

- **Incompatible management style** When the prevailing management style is at odds with an individual's personal style, it can be abrasive. A laid-back person will have just as many problems with an intense, hard-charging management style as an intense person will have with a laid-back approach.

- **Ongoing conflicts** Occasional personality clashes between people are normal, but a continuing confrontation will wear out even the most patient person. Be suspicious of people who are regularly involved in on-the-job upsets, regardless of whose "fault" the conflict is.

- **Quality-of-life issues** People are working to make a living— they have to have some time to live! Quality-of-life issues are becoming more important as workers realize there is more to happiness than just money. If your staff or management cannot have time to spend with their families, are unable to take a day off when they need it, or are burning themselves out routinely working 60 or more hours a week, they will eventually find another job.

- **Lack of control** This is a greater irritant at lower levels of the organization, but nobody likes to feel that they do not have any say in how their work environment operates.

- **Stress** When workers feel overwhelmed and out of control ("in the weeds"), the resulting stress makes productivity and responsive service impossible. There is a practical limit to how long anyone can operate effectively in this sort of environment.

- **Politics** In the absence of effective leadership, it is not uncommon for an operation to fragment into cliques. When playing the political game becomes more important than taking care of the guests, good workers will leave.

- **Pay versus effort** This problem arises when people feel that they are not getting paid enough for the level of work they are doing. It is an equity issue. Confronted with this problem, workers have three options: stay on the job and continue to harbor their resentment, reduce their output to a level they feel is justified by the pay, or seek another job.

- **Poor communication** When your staff is not "in on things" or does not know what is happening, their level of personal security goes down, they feel abandoned or unimportant, and they become disenchanted with the company.

- **Poor recruiting** The saying goes that "it is hard to fly with the eagles when you work with turkeys." If you fail to hire high-quality staff, you will discourage your better workers. Similarly, if you cannot fill vacancies and constantly require your staff to work short-handed, the good ones will inevitably head for the competition.

- **Lack of orientation** Workers who do not receive a thorough orientation to your company never fully understand the game or their place in it. Eventually they will quit out of frustration.

- **Lack of training** Failure to train your staff undermines their personal security and delivers a message that they are not very important to the success of your organization. If you don't care, why should they?

- **Ineffective supervision** To be effective, workers need direction, encouragement, feedback, and reinforcement. If supervisors allow policies to be broken, tolerate standards being compromised, or fail to act when action is needed, they lose the respect and support of the staff.

- **Lack of leadership** Leaders provide a shared vision and inspire their staff to accomplish things they didn't know they were capable of. Leadership is the glue that holds the staff together. All the management skills in the world cannot make up for lack of leadership.

- **Job inequities** Poverty is relative. The person with the least, no matter how much they have, always feels cheated. Typical job inequities are differing treatment of comparable workers with regard to pay, workload, or privileges.

- **Lack of management understanding** In this case, understanding deals with the depth of human feeling that managers bring to their work. Managers or supervisors who don't listen, show no compassion, or have no rapport with their crew will alienate people and drive them out of the company.

- **Boredom** Workers facing the same routine day after day will eventually be distracted by a lack of personal growth or development. This will not bother the poor performers, but the lack of professional challenge will push the good workers away.

- **Lack of job security** If workers do not feel that their jobs are relatively safe or that they may get "blind-sided" by a reactionary termination, they cannot make a long-term mental commitment to the company and its goals. This causes them to become increasingly estranged and feel "out of the loop." Productivity, guest service, and retention will suffer.

- **No opportunities for advancement** Exceptional performers need a sense of motion—a feeling that they are accomplishing something and improving themselves. This is usually demonstrated by their learning new skills and is reflected by their being promoted within the company when the opportunity arises. If qualified workers are not offered the first shot at job openings or if vacancies are routinely filled from outside the company, you will lose the good workers.

- **Not enough hours** People have to be able to make a living. If they cannot get enough hours to meet their expenses, they will have to take a second job or leave. A shortage of hours is particularly irritating when schedules reflect politics rather than performance.

- **Lack of benefits** Staff benefits, particularly health insurance, continues to be an issue in many parts of the foodservice industry, particularly among independent restaurants. At this writing, there is no nationally-mandated health-care coverage. For workers with families, the lack of employer-supported health insurance can be the factor that sends them looking for other employment.

- **High turnover** Interestingly, one of the principal causes for hourly workers leaving is high management turnover. A major reason departing managers give for leaving is high turnover among the staff! This is a situation that will only get worse if allowed to continue.

- **Lack of standards** The best workers have high professional standards. They will not long tolerate poor sanitation practices, lack of commitment to guest service, sloppy personal appearance, and so forth.

- **Lack of respect** You cannot build loyalty if you talk to your staff as though they were stupid, handle them like children, or treat them like potential criminals. If you find yourself habitually expecting the worst from your crew, you will probably get it!

- **Lack of feedback** You can't play to win if you don't know the score. High achievers always want to know the goal, how they are doing, and how they can do better. If your style is to look for problems and if your feedback to your staff is usually negative, you are part of the problem.

- **Sexual harassment** Sexual harassment is determined in the mind of the person who feels harassed. Just because you do not believe you have sexist attitudes or policies does not mean that others will not have adverse reactions to your choice of words, gestures, jokes, uniforms, and so forth.

- **Racism** This is another type of unequal treatment. Understand that many minorities are often extremely sensitive to behavior and attitudes that seem to them to be racially influenced. Whether or not their interpretation is accurate from your perspective, you must be sensitive to the fact that racism, like sexual harassment, is determined in the mind of the person who feels discriminated against.

- **Personal reasons** Several reasons for leaving are, in fact, personal. It is not unusual for people to move out of the area, decide to change careers, graduate from school, retire, or decide to devote more time to their families. Be warned, however, that "personal reasons" can be a catch-all category that departing staff may cite to avoid a confrontation with management when their real reason for leaving comes under one of the previous categories discussed.

EXIT INTERVIEWS

An inexpensive but very effective way to keep a finger on the pulse of the organization is to conduct exit interviews whenever a staff member leaves. Smart operators regularly ask their guests how they could do a better job for them next time because the feedback, however unpleasant, helps them improve. Similarly, why not ask departing staff members what changes they would suggest to make the organization a better place to work?

The problem is that workers are most likely to be leaving because of something management did, something management allowed to happen, or because management did not listen to them. If people felt the company did not listen to them while they were on the staff, they probably won't feel like telling the company much when they leave. That's the problem of working for people who don't listen! Still, the feedback is essential.

If you want to get the information, you may need someone outside the company who is "safe" to talk to and who will respect the confidentiality of the departing worker. Large multi-unit operators may have a personnel department that can handle this function effectively. Smaller operators, however, often have to find another way.

One possibility might be to hire someone on an "as needed" basis to interview departing staff members. The most effective interviewer will be someone the staff did not have regular contact with during a typical workday. Perhaps you know of a retiree in the area or perhaps a former worker who resigned to raise a family. Often these people would like a little social contact and a few extra dollars. The advantage of one-on-one exit interviews is that they are more personal and a skillful interviewer can often get past the departing person's natural defensiveness to uncover the real reasons behind their decision to leave. The disadvantages are that not all interviewers are effective and the personal interview approach requires coordinating the departing worker's schedule with the availability of the interviewer.

Another alternative for many independent operators and small chains is to use blind exit questionnaires directed to an impartial third party who conveys the responses anonymously to the company. This arrangement saves you adding another person to your payroll and avoids the schedule coordination required with one-on-one interviews. The disadvantage is that you lose the ability for follow-up questions and clarification of answers. Still, *any* information is better than none. In researching this approach to exit interviewing, I did not find an organization that was providing this service to the industry—so I started one myself! Figure 1-1 is a sample of the exit interview questionnaire I developed for Hospitality Service Group, a third-party intermediary that collects and forwards survey results from departing staff members. The material is copyrighted, but as a purchaser of this book, you have permission to use it in your own operation.

FOCUS ON THE SYSTEM, NOT THE PEOPLE

Receiving this feedback will not make any difference unless you use it to gain insights into the way you do business and utilize it to make positive adjustments in your organization. After all, if nothing changes, nothing is going to change.

We all like to think that everything we do is working, that our

©1995, Hospitality Service Group
CC:

HOSPITALITY SERVICE GROUP
PO Box 280 · Gig Harbor, WA 98335
(800) 767-1055

STAFF QUESTIONNAIRE

Why did you leave? ☐ I Quit ☐ I Was Fired ☐ My Temporary Job Ended ☐ _____
Where did you usually work? ☐ Dining Room ☐ Kitchen ☐ Bar ☐ Management ☐ Office/Admin ☐ _____
Did you typically work ☐ Full Time or ☐ Part Time?
Was your departure a surprise to you? ☐ Yes ☐ No   Do you think your departure a surprise to the company? ☐ Yes ☐ No

A number of things can happen at work that may cause people to think about leaving their jobs. Mark an "X" in the box that shows how much you agree or disagree with each of these statements about what it was like to work for this company.   STRONGLY AGREE << >> STRONGLY DISAGREE

1. There was too much turnover in the company ☐ ☐ ☐ ☐ ☐
2. There was little or no feeling of teamwork ☐ ☐ ☐ ☐ ☐
3. My manager's/supervisor's style was very different from mine ☐ ☐ ☐ ☐ ☐
4. There were too many on-the-job conflicts that stayed unresolved ☐ ☐ ☐ ☐ ☐
5. I couldn't get time off when I needed it ☐ ☐ ☐ ☐ ☐

6. I had to work too many hours ☐ ☐ ☐ ☐ ☐
7. I could not get as many hours as I needed ☐ ☐ ☐ ☐ ☐
8. I had nothing to say about how things were done ☐ ☐ ☐ ☐ ☐
9. There was too much job-related stress ☐ ☐ ☐ ☐ ☐
10. There was too much company politics ☐ ☐ ☐ ☐ ☐

11. The pay was too low for the amount of work I was asked to do ☐ ☐ ☐ ☐ ☐
12. Communication in the company was poor ☐ ☐ ☐ ☐ ☐
13. My co-workers were not very qualified for their jobs ☐ ☐ ☐ ☐ ☐
14. I never really understood my job or the company ☐ ☐ ☐ ☐ ☐
15. I did not receive any real training ☐ ☐ ☐ ☐ ☐

16. The training I received was inconsistent or worthless ☐ ☐ ☐ ☐ ☐
17. My managers/supervisors were not very effective ☐ ☐ ☐ ☐ ☐
18. There was a general lack of leadership in the company ☐ ☐ ☐ ☐ ☐
19. People were not being treated equally or fairly ☐ ☐ ☐ ☐ ☐
20. My managers/supervisors didn't listen to me ☐ ☐ ☐ ☐ ☐

21. My managers/supervisors took no personal interest in my success ☐ ☐ ☐ ☐ ☐
22. My job was boring ☐ ☐ ☐ ☐ ☐
23. There was no job security ☐ ☐ ☐ ☐ ☐
24. There was no opportunity for advancement ☐ ☐ ☐ ☐ ☐
25. The professional standards of the company were low ☐ ☐ ☐ ☐ ☐

26. I didn't feel that anyone appreciated the work that I did ☐ ☐ ☐ ☐ ☐
27. I didn't trust my managers/supervisors ☐ ☐ ☐ ☐ ☐
28. I was concerned for my personal safety while at work ☐ ☐ ☐ ☐ ☐
29. People were regularly working under the influence of drugs or alcohol ☐ ☐ ☐ ☐ ☐
30. My managers/supervisors were very moody ☐ ☐ ☐ ☐ ☐

31. My managers/supervisors never asked for my opinions about anything ☐ ☐ ☐ ☐ ☐
32. My managers/supervisors never told me how I was doing ☐ ☐ ☐ ☐ ☐
33. I was treated disrespectfully by my managers/supervisors ☐ ☐ ☐ ☐ ☐
34. I ran into racist attitudes or practices ☐ ☐ ☐ ☐ ☐
35. I ran into sexual harassment or sexist attitudes ☐ ☐ ☐ ☐ ☐

36. I am moving out of the area ☐ ☐ ☐ ☐ ☐
37. I am changing careers ☐ ☐ ☐ ☐ ☐
38. I am graduating from school ☐ ☐ ☐ ☐ ☐
39. I am retiring ☐ ☐ ☐ ☐ ☐
40. My family obligations demanded more of my time ☐ ☐ ☐ ☐ ☐

To receive the $5.00 reward, just answer all the questions on this side of the form.

Figure 1-1   Sample Exit Interview Questionnaire

Questions on this side of the form are optional. You can answer them or not, but your comments will be extremely valuable.

What did you like *most* about working for this company?

_____
_____
_____
_____
_____
_____
_____

What did you like *least* about working for this company?

_____
_____
_____
_____
_____
_____
_____

If this were your company, what would you change about it?

_____
_____
_____
_____
_____
_____
_____

Is there anything else you want to tell the company?

_____
_____
_____
_____
_____
_____
_____
_____

Thank you for your comments and suggestions

Figure 1-1 (*continued*)

staff understands our intent, and that we are good operators. Finding out that people are leaving because of something we are doing (or not doing) can be a knife in the heart. Like guest complaints, these insights are difficult messages to receive without an emotional reaction. For your own sanity, I caution you to look for failures in the system, not for failures in people.

Here's an example of another type of operating problem we often face that will illustrate what I mean: Let's say you have a standard that food orders should be up within fifteen minutes of the time they are placed because you have determined that fifteen minutes is the time it takes to meet your guests' needs and expectations. Harry is working the pantry and is concerned that orders often take 20 minutes or more to get out of his station. He comes to you and reports the delays.

If you look for people failures, it would be easy to blame Harry. If, when he reports the delay, you say something like "Thanks for telling me that, Harry. There obviously is a problem here and I think you are the problem. Since you seem unable to meet our standards, you're fired!" Don't laugh. Variations on this scene happen all the time. If you chose to deal with it this way, the one thing you could count on is that this is probably the last time *anyone* on your staff would ever tell you about an operating problem! Guest service would suffer, your conscientious workers would be more likely to become disenchanted, and it would eventually show up as lowered morale and increased turnover.

On the other hand, if you were to stay focused on system failures, you would greet Harry's report with enthusiasm and gratitude; enthusiasm because he was taking responsibility for the success of the operation and gratitude because he had provided an insight into where the operation was breaking down and how you might be able to deliver a better level of service to your guests.

You might then explore with Harry where the system is weak. Perhaps the menu is heavy on pantry items and the station is overloaded. Maybe there are some items that are so complicated to prepare that no one could get them out on time. A needed piece of equipment might be missing or broken. It could be that the service staff doesn't know how to use the POS system. Perhaps orders are not very clear when they come in and it takes a lot of additional discussion with the service staff to sort it out.

Even if the problem truly lies with Harry's inability to perform, was he properly trained? Does he understand what he has to do and how to do it? If Harry is definitely the wrong person for that particular job, how was he assigned to it? If Harry shouldn't be working for you at all, where did the staff selection system break down so that he was hired in the first place?

I think you get the point. It is easy to blame individuals for your operational problems, but it is never productive. The problem is never with your people. All they did was ask for a job—*you* are the one that gave it to them!

You will also find that when you look for system failures, it becomes safe for your existing staff to talk to you about problems in the operation. Few of your staff will "rat" on their co-workers because they figure that management's job is to know what's going on. No one will report a problem that is a result of personal inability to perform in a situation where that will be professional suicide.

By eagerly seeking out breakdowns in the system, you become much more approachable. This attitude will encourage everyone in the company to be part of the solution because they get rewarded (with your appreciation) for identifying areas that could be working better. In addition to creating a smoother-running organization, you also foster teamwork and job involvement. People will be more inclined to stay and help fix things than to leave out of frustration.

Chapter Two

Think in Terms of Retention

How I am working on a problem often indicates how I am keeping it a problem.

—Hugh Prather

You have probably seen or heard of studies on human behavior suggesting that what you think about is what you tend to get. This means that if you want to do better at keeping people, you have to think about the people who are staying (retention) rather than focusing on the people you are losing (turnover).

WHO ARE THE PEOPLE WHO STAY?

Workers who stay fit into four general groups, categorized by their motives and the length of time they stay.

- **Wanderers** are people who traditionally come and go. They are transients with short-term goals, usually financial, and they will work only as long as necessary to get the money for their next step. Foodservice positions are often particularly attractive to this group. Wanderers may be high school or college students, military personnel, housewives, or moonlighters with a mission. They may be good workers, but they are not actively looking for a foodservice career. If you hire them, expect to lose them when their immediate needs have been met.

- **Fillers** are workers who are basically unhappy but stay anyway. These folks don't make waves, have little interest in advancement, and produce just enough to keep from getting fired. They have essentially retired on the job.

- **Achievers** are the people who enjoy the job and work for the challenge, not the money. These workers are motivated by the opportunity to grow. They get restless and leave when their personal and professional development stagnates. Achievers will demand your best efforts and can make a valuable contribution to your operation for as long as you can keep them interested.

- **Keepers** stay because they like their work and enjoy being part of the company. If you treat them right, they will brighten your day, make your guests happy, and build your bottom line. Solid, successful organizations are built from keepers.

The long-term success of your company will certainly be built on the achievers and the keepers, some of whom can slide into the category of fillers if you get complacent and start taking your business for granted. Wanderers fill in the gaps, take up the seasonal slack, and bring some new perspectives to the operation.

At any given time, your organization will have people in all these categories. It will help your composure to have an idea of who is who. While you must be careful of stereotyping, having some understanding of the motives of each person on your staff can be helpful. For example, you would not typically expect wanderers to show much commitment to long-term projects. To enlist their support, you must show them how the success of the project will benefit them in their future pursuits outside the company. Fillers are unlikely to be interested in any sort of change or challenge. When you know who has retired on the job, don't waste time getting upset at their lack of response and start to gently move them out of the organization.[1] Be sure to keep challenging the achievers by giving them new projects

[1]For some help on how to do this, refer to the results-based position descriptions in *The Foolproof Foodservice Selection System*.

and responsibilities. The keepers just need your sincere appreciation and an increasing role in the decision-making process.

THE SIMPLE ROOT OF TURNOVER

Once you find the right people—the achievers and the keepers—you have to keep them. High staff turnover has been the curse of the foodservice industry. To achieve our professional goals, we must do a more effective job of keeping the wonderful people we spend so much time selecting. It sounds simplistic to say, but *your staff leaves because they do not want to stay!*

To slow down the revolving door, it helps to shift your focus and start thinking in terms of retention instead of turnover. Limiting your thinking to turnover will keep your attention on the number of people leaving. When you start looking at your business in terms of retention, you start concentrating on the percentage of the staff that stays. The distinction may seem like a semantic exercise, but the change in emphasis is an important first step in regaining control.

WHAT IS TURNOVER AND WHAT ISN'T?

The typical industry definition of turnover is the number of people on the payroll over the year (the number of W-2 forms issued) divided by the average number of people on the staff. The flaw in this formula is that it creates an artificially high number that may condition foodservice managers to accept the revolving door as inevitable. Having been numbed to their inability to influence their retention rate, many managers don't even try.

The problem with this definition is that nobody stays forever. Sooner or later, for one reason or another, everyone in your organization will leave. Some will quit, some will be fired, and a few may even be around long enough to retire. The traditional definition of turnover does not allow for planned seasonal staff build-ups and scale-downs, does not make a distinction between full-time and part-time workers, and does not consider the length of time departing workers have been with the company or their reasons for leaving.

Since everyone leaves eventually, not every departure should count as turnover. Would you be bothered if someone quits after working with you for six years? Are you surprised when students leave after graduation? What about the serviceman's wife who resigns when her husband gets new orders? These are just facts of life, not turnover problems.

So in an effort to come up with a statistic that more truly represents the retention climate of the operation, let me offer a revised definition of turnover for our industry:

> Turnover is losing people you did not want to lose when you did not expect to lose them.

Since that definition by itself is difficult to quantify, perhaps it will help to look at the specific parameters that make it up:

Turnover *is*:

- **Resignations with less than two weeks' notice** Employees who abandon their jobs (no show, no call) or leave with less than two weeks' notice are delivering a message. If the working environment in your operation is so oppressive that good workers lose faith, get angry, or care so little about the company that they would knowingly leave you hanging, it will show up in this category.

- **Terminations (except temporary staff)** When workers do not succeed in their jobs and termination is the only recourse, the problem can be attributed to one of two possibilities: either there is a breakdown in the staff selection procedure and you are accepting unqualified applicants, or the quality of the working environment, professional training, and staff development (coaching) is suspect.

- **Any regular staff resignation within the first six months** Selecting the right people and being properly committed to their training and success will not guarantee that they will stay forever, but they should want to keep their jobs longer than six months. If not, it is a comment you should not ignore.

Turnover *is not*:

- **Resignations with more than two weeks' notice** Everyone on your staff will eventually leave the company. When workers give you plenty of advance notice, it shows that they have respect for, and feel some identity with, the organization. The longer the notice they give, the more positive the comment.
- **Planned release of temporary staff** Temporary workers are hired for a specific period of time, usually to cover seasonal surges in business. Since their departure is planned from the outset, it is not a comment on management when it happens and should not properly be counted as turnover.

In addition, turnover should be figured on the basis of full-time equivalents (FTEs) to more fairly consider the total labor required to operate the restaurant and avoid penalizing operators for hiring part-time workers over full-timers.

IS TURNOVER A BAD THING?

A certain amount of turnover is normal and healthy. Without some influx of new talent and ideas, it is easy for an operation to get stale. The goal of a successful retention program is not zero turnover. After all, we don't want people to retire on the job! The primary intent of a retention program is to be sure you don't lose your truly great workers—the achievers and the keepers—unexpectedly.

In an ideal world, you would never hire anyone who was not a top-quality candidate (and if you follow *The Foolproof Foodservice Selection System*[2], you will greatly increase your odds of doing just that). However, not all good-looking candidates will live up to their potential. Good operators will also make sure that they *do* lose workers who do not perform to their standards, so a successful retention program should also help identify marginal performers and help them leave the organization.

HOW DO YOU KEEP SCORE?

As we said, what gets measured is what gets done. You can look at retention either in a specific or a general way. When looking at specific aspects of retention, consider the average tenure by position. How long do workers in each particular category stay now? How long would you *like* them to stay? Once you know these statistics, set a target and consider anything less as turnover.

In your general monitoring of staff retention, I suggest you start keeping the Staff Retention Worksheet included as Figure 2-1. This form can be kept on a weekly or monthly basis. The worksheet is self-explanatory and its regular use will start to give you a handle on your retention performance. There are no particular "right numbers," but having a standard format will start to show whether your retention rate is improving or getting worse.

In addition to statistics, any review of staff retention should consider whether resignations were for reasons over which the company had control or whether they perhaps indicate weaknesses that should have been caught during the selection process. The goal is not necessarily to achieve a specific statistical result, but to use the statistical results as a means to improve the work environment. For example, the Staff Retention Worksheet asks you to note which

[2]Bill Marvin, *The Foolproof Foodservice Selection System,* John Wiley & Sons, Inc., 1993.

STAFF RETENTION WORKSHEET

FTE on Payroll (at start of Period): _____   Period _____   Prepared by _____   Date _____

NAME OF DEPARTED WORKER	LENGTH OF SVC	FTE *	#WKS NOTICE -2 2-4 4+	COACH/MENTOR OF DEPARTED WORKER	REPLACED INT EXT	DEPARTED WORKER REPLACED BY	COACH/MENTOR OF REPLACEMENT
TERMINATION 1.	mo		☐ ☐ ☐		☐ ☐		
2.	mo		☐ ☐ ☐		☐ ☐		
3.	mo		☐ ☐ ☐		☐ ☐		
4.	mo		☐ ☐ ☐		☐ ☐		
5.	mo		☐ ☐ ☐		☐ ☐		
6.	mo		☐ ☐ ☐		☐ ☐		
RESIGNATION 1.	mo		☐ ☐ ☐		☐ ☐		
2.	mo		☐ ☐ ☐		☐ ☐		
3.	mo		☐ ☐ ☐		☐ ☐		
4.	mo		☐ ☐ ☐		☐ ☐		
5.	mo		☐ ☐ ☐		☐ ☐		
6.	mo		☐ ☐ ☐		☐ ☐		
TRANSFER 1.	mo				☐ ☐		
2.	mo				☐ ☐		
3.	mo				☐ ☐		
4.	mo				☐ ☐		
5.	mo				☐ ☐		
6.	mo				☐ ☐		

* Average schedule of 10 hr/wk or less = .25 FTE; 11-20 hrs/wk = .50 FTE; 21-30 hrs/wk = .75 FTE; 31+hrs/wk = 1.00 FTE

FTE Resigns (-2 wk notice) + _____ FTE Departed (-6 mos svc) not previously counted = TURNOVER

FTE Term + _____ FTE Resigns (-2 wk notice) + _____ FTE Departed (-6 mos svc) not previously counted = TURNOVER

(_____ FTE on Payroll - _____ Turnover) / _____ FTE on Payroll = RETENTION RATE

	THIS PERIOD	LAST PERIOD	TARGET
	%	%	%

Figure 2-1   Staff Retention Worksheet

vacancies were filled by internal promotion or internal transfer. When a job opening comes up, an excellent organization will have well-trained individuals ready to move into positions of greater responsibility[3].

---

[3]See Chapter 8, "Create a Sense of Motion."

Part Two
Recognize the Roots

Chapter Three

Improve Your Understanding of People

We conferred endlessly and futilely and arrived at the place from whence we began. Then we did what we knew we had to do in the first place, and we failed as we knew we would.

—attributed to Sir Winston Churchill

Whether the opening quote is accurate or not, the thought behind it deserves consideration. Are we spending our time becoming incredibly adept at ineffective procedures? Have you ever thought that there *had* to be a better way to deal with operational issues than the way you learned? Does the idea that you have to work 60 or more hours a week to succeed in foodservice strike you as a suspicious notion?

Solving operating problems in the wide world of foodservice can often seem like trying to write your name in the sand! Operational issues exist in a fluid environment that has an endless array of variables, so the answers are never very clear or permanent. Add to that the variety of different operating headaches and it is easy to become overwhelmed by details.

Keeping current on this minutiae is exhausting. Most operators put in long hours and apply themselves with good intention, but they are seldom as effective over the long term as they would like to

be. Even when everything is done "right" and there is some immediate improvement, we rarely create a solution that will stay in place
without continual attention.

The reason we have had such fleeting success with operating
problems is that we often place our emphasis in the wrong places.
Following established tradition, we attack issues with professional
expertise and techniques. This deals with the symptoms well
enough but does nothing to address the human factors that create
the problems in the first place. Turnover is no different.

No matter what the specific symptoms, the common denomina-
tor of all foodservice problems is people. People cause all the problems and people ultimately have to be part of any lasting solution.
Yet few managers have ever had any real training in what makes
people tick. The closest I ever came to gaining such knowledge was
in a high school psychology course. I learned about paranoid schizo-
phrenics and manic-depressives, but no one ever really taught me
about normal people.

When you think about it, most people become supervisors by de-
cree. "You've been here the longest (you have a degree, your family
owns the place, and so forth) so you'll be the new supervisor. Go
supervise." The difficulty is that the popular model of management
is a lot closer to law enforcement than it is to enlightened leadership. Not an exciting thought, is it? If you had wanted a career in
law enforcement, you could have gone to the Police Academy—at
least you would be able to carry a gun when you finished!

Following the cop model, we try to force our staff to do what we
want them to do. Most of what passes for management is little more
than advanced manipulation. The frustrating part is that we expect
that it will work. In fact, being a cop is seldom effective in the long
run because it does not properly address the human factor and *every*
operating problem, including turnover, is just a "people problem"
in disguise.

My favorite swamp philosopher, the cartoon character Pogo, once
observed that "We have met the enemy and it is us!" This suggests
that the problems we are dealing with are problems of our own cre-
ation. We have the problems we have because of the way we have
decided to do things. Sometimes these are conscious decisions; often

they are not. However, if we are the cause of our own problems, then we are also the source of their solution. After all, we can change, and changing ourselves is a lot more controllable (and a lot more likely) than trying to get *someone else* to change!

Before you take yourself to task for creating a lot of problems for yourself, there is some news of two sorts that you must consider:

> THE GOOD NEWS: Seeing things the way you do, you couldn't possibly do what you are doing any other way than the way you are.

The truth of it is that we do the things we do because they make sense to us. Even the things that don't work are done because we think they will (or should) solve our need of the moment. The difficulty, of course, is that if we are not getting the results we want with our present operating approach, doing more of it is not likely to improve our effectiveness.

> THE BAD NEWS: Doing more of what you've been doing will only get you more of what you've got!

If your thinking doesn't change, nothing is going to change. That sounds simple enough. But change—even change for the better—is usually traumatic.

> THE GOOD NEWS: When you see things differently, everything changes naturally.

Fortunately, because people always do what makes sense to them, acquiring a fresh perspective changes everything. You will still do what makes sense to you, but because you see things in a different way, your reaction (and your results) will be different. You may not even notice the shift, but your staff will.

Everyone says that foodservice is a "people business," but from whom did we ever really learn about people or how to supervise them? I suspect that the most common way we learned was by following the model set by our previous superiors. "Find things that are wrong and fix them" is still typically the order of the day. If you want to spend the rest of your life looking for the dark side of things, this style will work perfectly. The problem, of course, is that it really doesn't work—an unfortunate circumstance that many ascribe to the poor quality of today's workers rather than to the inherent unworkability of the "cop" mode of management.

Are we really just getting better and better at doing things that don't work? If so, how can we start to unravel things? In Chapter 4 we will look at organizations and suggest some ways to create a more productive working environment. But for now, let's start by taking a fresh look at people as individuals.

To get the most from the notions that follow in the next two chapters, I suggest four things:

1. **Suspend judgment.** Resist the urge to decide point by point whether you agree or disagree with what I am suggesting. You are welcome to accept or reject these ideas at any time so there's no pressure. Suspending judgment for awhile will allow you to consider some new views without their having to align with anything you already believe.

2. **Read softly.** When you read softly, you are looking more for the spirit of the material rather than for any hard facts. Your goal is understanding, not knowledge. The only quiz on this material will be answered by your success in your relationships with others.

3. **Be curious.** Roll these ideas around in your mind a bit and ponder how they might apply. Question whether you might be exhibiting any of these behaviors. Speculate how various situations in your past might have turned out differently had you approached them in a different way. You don't need to draw any conclusions, just consider the possibilities.

4. **Validate from your own experience.** Look into your own

experiences to confirm whether what these views suggest about people really describe the way people work. We have a tendency to want to make life more complicated than it needs to be.

WHAT MAKES PEOPLE TICK?

If you understand the following five specific aspects of people, you will be more effective in dealing with your staff (or your boss, your family, your guests, your suppliers . . .):

1. Presence
2. State of mind
3. Personal cultures
4. Tone of voice
5. Personal example

Let's examine these areas in more detail:

1. *Presence*

The secret to creating impact with others is presence. Simply put,

> Presence is a state of mind that is free from distraction.

Your level of presence is the extent to which your mind is not occupied with thoughts unrelated to the project at hand.

Here are a few examples of what I mean. Have you ever been talking to someone who was listening to you . . . and then suddenly they *weren't* listening to you? They may even have been looking at you and nodding their heads as you spoke, but don't you know when their attention was elsewhere? Have you talked with someone on the phone while they were doing something else at the same time? Even though you can't see them, hasn't it been obvious when you don't have their total attention? These are both instances of distraction or low presence. Now recall your experience of what it feels like to talk to someone who wasn't really listening to you. If you are like most people, you probably find the behavior to be rude at best and angering at worst.

> A distracted state of mind causes other people to disconnect from you.

It is incredibly annoying to talk with someone whose mind has wandered, and yet we do the same thing to people constantly. Somehow we've accepted the notion that trying to do several tasks at once is the way to be efficient and get more done. In fact, the truth may be just the opposite. Have you ever listened to the phone with one ear while you were working on the schedule and trying to handle a staff member's question at the same time? This is a typical scene in foodservice. My guess is that neither the person on the other end of the phone, nor the schedule, nor the staff member got the quality of attention they really needed, and that you likely had to go back to one or all of these "projects" for clarification or to give it a second try.

Managers who are honest with themselves recognize that they can really only concentrate on one thing at a time anyway. When you are talking with someone, there is little you can do about finishing the schedule (or your food cost, your sick child, or your vacation). The secret to productivity is to drop distractions, handle one item at a time with maximum presence, and move on to the next project. The lack of distraction will enable you to more accurately assess the situation and quickly deal with it in an effective way.

When your guests have a complaint or when members of your staff have a question or a problem, what they want most is to feel that you really *heard* what they had to say. Most people do not expect you to resolve their concerns on the spot, but they want to sense that what they had to say was important to you. You convey your level of caring by your level of presence. If you are distracted, people do not *feel* listened to and will continue to voice their concerns until either they feel you got the message or they give up on you. (By the way, when they give up on you, they will probably leave for another job!) If you have ever worked for someone who did not listen, you know the feeling of being ignored. Just be sure that you are not guilty of the same sin when someone needs your attention.

> Presence draws people to a more positive state of mind.

While a distracted state of mind creates irritation, presence makes people feel more positive. Presence is not something unnatural—all of us are born with presence. Little babies have very high presence because their heads aren't yet cluttered with thoughts. Babies only known how to deal with what is in front of them at the moment. Think of the effect when you bring a baby into the room. All attention shifts to the baby, people start to smile and forget about their own problems for a few minutes. The baby isn't *doing* anything except just being there. This demonstrates the power presence has to make others feel more positive. High presence is our birthright, but it is also something we can lose sight of as our lives became increasingly complex and we take on "responsiblities."

It is unrealistic to think that we can always operate without distractions, but we can at least start to be aware of distracting thoughts when they start to clutter our minds. One way to tell that this is happening is when people you are talking with start to get restless or when you see a glazed look in their eyes. If your attention wanders, so will theirs. When you find yourself distracted, drop whatever stray thoughts are in your head and bring your attention back to the task at hand. Your increased presence will make your audience feel better and bring more impact to your message.

2. State of Mind

The key to truly understanding people and why they do what they do lies in grasping the power of state of mind. State of mind might be called your level of well-being, your feeling of personal security, or your mood. For example, being in love is a very high state of mind, whereas being angry is a very low one.

Our view of the world changes as our moods change. You know from personal experience that when you are having a bad day, *everything* is a disaster! Conversely, when you feel wonderful, the whole world just works more easily for you. The events of the day don't change, but their impact changes significantly.

In a low state of mind, the world looks pretty threatening. Every event you face seems like a threat. You are apt to be depressed, hostile, or scared. You probably feel highly disconnected from life. As your level of personal security rises, your outlook improves, and you might find that you are just irritable. At this level of thinking, you tend to be critical, impatient, and distant. You find yourself easily distracted and have a hard time focussing. You are, however, becoming more involved in what is going on around you. For some people, irritable is about as good as it gets!

A step above irritation is a state of mind where you feel engaged in the events of your life. You may be fairly neutral about what is happening around you—you might say you are apathetic or even bored. Life is not bad, but it probably does not seem very exciting, either. Respect and exhilaration are still higher states of mind. You may have experienced a state approaching joy when you were in love. At these higher levels, you are able to take life as it comes without a problem. You have a natural appreciation for the world around you and find that you have an instinctive knack for being with people. Exceptional service happens almost automatically when you are in a high state of mind because you are naturally compassionate and genuinely want to take care of others.

Here's another way to think of the relationship between state of mind and your thoughts. Most lakes and ponds are beautiful. But if you drop the water level about ten feet, you are going to see a lot of debris. There are rocks, logs, bottles and who knows what else under the surface. If the level drops, you can spend days, even months, trying to clean up the bottom of the lake and you won't make a noticeable difference. If you allow the water level to rise, however, the lake will be beautiful again. All the junk is still down there, but it is no longer an issue.

People are the same way. When their level of well-being drops, they can do, say or think any number of ugly things. This ugliness will always exist at low levels—you can't clean it up. However, when someone's level of personal security rises, all the unpleasantness just disappears naturally. It may still be down there, but it is not an issue. Understand that a healthy state of mind is the natural condition.

A person's state of mind determines how the world looks to them, which in turn determines their behavior. Once you grasp this idea, you will start to realize something remarkable:

> Behavior is only a symptom of a person's state of mind.

The concept is so simple and yet revolutionary when we compare it to the way we always thought things worked. Let me describe a personal example to illustrate the power of this understanding.

. . . it was one of *those* days!

In the mid-1980s, I was hired by the United States Olympic Committee to manage over the foodservice at the Olympic Training Center (OTC) in Colorado Springs. The OTC was an ongoing operation whose dining program was in need of major surgery. In fact, the foodservice had consistently been the leading source of complaints from the athletes about their training experience.

To underscore how bad things were, the day I arrived to take over the dining operations we had two knife fights in the kitchen! Two of my kitchen crew had gotten into an argument and had attempted to resolve it by waving french knives at each other with some degree of seriousness. No damage was done, but the event had everyone nervous for a few minutes.

I had received some excellent training up to that point in my professional career, but nowhere was there any instruction in how to deal with knife fights! Needless to say, this had all the signs of being a real "Day from Hell"! I hope you never encounter a predicament like this in your own operation but it could be an interesting case study. For a moment, put yourself in my position and imagine how you might have approached this situation.

In the old "management expertise" mode that I spent so many years refining, my first response to this predicament would likely have been to fire—or least suspend or put on probation—the people involved. After all, it is important to deliver a clear message that this is unacceptable behavior.

After that, if I didn't already have one, I would have written a clear policy about knife fights. The policy would have specified that engaging in such dangerous behavior was unacceptable conduct and could be considered grounds for immediate dismissal. Just to be sure the point wasn't lost, the agreement not to engage in knife fights might even have been one of those statements that all staff members are required to sign when they join the company.

Finally, I would have held a special staff meeting to explain the policy. I would be sure my staff understood how behavior of this sort worked against everything we were trying to accomplish in the operation. I would have talked about the importance of teamwork and cooperation, probably with some analogies from the Olympic games. I would have shared my vision for the operation and tried to get my crew excited about what we could do together. It would have been an inspirational session designed to help my staff see that we were all in this together and we had to work together to succeed in providing memorable service to the athletes.

In my seminars, I have shared this story with operators across North America. As we reach this point in the discussion, the majority of managers generally agree that they would take an approach similar to the traditional strategy just described. Assuming you were confronted with this problem, is this about the way you would handle it?

My next question to them (and to you) is this:

"How effective do you think this strategy would be in eliminating knife fights forever and always in your operation?"

Somewhat red-faced, the managers usually confess that while there might be some short-term effect, they don't really expect much would change.

"Is this more or less what you would do?"

"Well . . . yes."

"Would it work?"

"Well . . . no."

"But it's still about the way you would handle it?"

"Well . . . yes."

Do you see the problem? Now had I followed this scenario, my strategy would not have worked either. Worse yet, when I didn't get the results I wanted, my approach would have been to figure out how to write a better policy or how to hold a better staff meeting! I would worry that perhaps I didn't come down on them fast enough and hard enough. It would never have occurred to me that approaching the problem in this manner was a futile exercise from the very beginning. This is what I mean about becoming better and better at doing things that don't work!

When the knife fights came up, however, I had a different understanding about the real cause of behavior. I had started to recognize that behavior was just a symptom of a person's level of thinking. Instead of seeing the knife fights as a statement about the people involved, I saw the incident as an indication of a low level of personal security. The workers involved in the incident were simply in a state of mind where swinging knives at each other seemed like an appropriate way to settle a dispute. I understood that the only way the behavior would change would be to change the thinking that created it.

In this case, I talked with the combatants and probably suggested that carving up their co-workers was inappropriate and dangerous, but I never addressed the fight directly. Instead, my conversation probably went something like this:

"Given what happened, it is obvious to me that something has you really frustrated. What's wrong with this chicken outfit? What's making your job tough and what do you think we can do about it?"

My goal was to get an insight into what was weighing heavily on the minds of my crew because whatever it was, it was making their lives difficult, affecting their thinking and leading to their unproductive behavior. Accomplishing this goal required that I listen without judgement because that is a major aid in helping move people to a healthier state of mind. All it would take for them to change their behavior was that they increase their level of personal security and well-being to a point where they would not even think seriously of making a personal attack on someone.

One of the first things I learned was that we had twice as many people on the staff as we needed. At that time, activity at the OTC was very seasonal and my predecessor had not dismissed any of the additional workers that were hired to handle the summer business. It was November, the athlete count was low, and everyone was working half hours. They were not making enough money to live on, but they could not afford to quit. I would have been frustrated, too!

After a series of one-on-one interviews to get some sense of my new workers, I fired half of them! I placed on my termination list those whom I believed were the most negative or angry, but even if everyone had been in a great mood, I *still* would have let half of them go. After the initial shock, everyone immediately felt better because the negative people were gone and all those who remained had a full schedule. The question of adequate hours having been eliminated, the general climate improved and people were more inclined to suggest other areas that could be corrected. Every time we uncovered an irritant, we fixed it, and the climate steadily became more positive.

Some interesting things happened. A few days later, not only had the knife fights stopped, but the very idea of swinging a knife at someone wouldn't even enter anyone's mind! In fact, we never talked about knife fights again and we never had a similar incident in the five years I was with the OTC.

There were some other interesting benefits of this approach: Within about two months, OTC foodservice had become the number one source of compliments from the athletes and coaches—all the more remarkable when you consider that this happened with essentially the same workers who had made us the number one source of complaints. Over the next six months, dining room patronage (the number of meals eaten per athlete day) nearly doubled while the cost per meal dropped over 20 percent. Staff turnover went from 300 percent to 25 percent without a change in wage rates. I resigned almost five years later because I had accomplished everything I had hoped to achieve at the OTC. There was nothing left for me to do because my staff was really running things. Most gratifying, the people involved in the knife fights were still on staff and were among our most productive workers.

A person's state of mind also determines how the person handles the everyday ravages of life. Human relations consultant Robert Kausen gives the following example:

> *Imagine that you and your employees are making an ocean voyage in small sail boats. If the seas are calm, each sailor can manage his or her boat fairly well. Some will be more expert than others but none will get into serious difficulty. Now suppose that a weather system develops; winds pick up and swells increase. The expert sailors enjoy the change while the novices become tense and worried. If a full storm develops, the experts will be challenged just to keep from swamping while the less experienced may capsize and drown. Under these conditions, completing the journey, let alone enjoying it, is lost to the needs of pure survival.*

In a high state of mind, everybody is an expert sailor on the seas of life. In a low state of mind, we are all novices.

What changes the level?

We have discussed how a person's level of personal security (mood, state of mind, and so forth) determines how the world looks to them and how their thinking, in turn, determines their behavior. At this point it might be productive to review a few common management practices that can affect an individual's sense of well-being. Here are a few suggestions:

1. **Compliments/Criticism**   Compliments tend to make people feel better whereas criticism brings them down. Don't you

just *love* to be criticized? In practice, most managers tend to reprimand workers for those things that are being done incorrectly rather than praising them for those things that are being done right. Now if someone is about to strike a guest or cut off their finger, immediate, decisive action is definitely needed. But people do what they are rewarded for and one of the most potent rewards you have to give is your attention and encouragement. Take a look at your operation and see if your system is built on rewards for doing things right or punishments for doing things wrong. The real key to effectiveness is neutrality—placing no more energy on things done right than you do on things done incorrectly. People will still respond more favorably to the good news, but you will create a more adult relationship if you minimize any drama.

2. **Good Health/Physical Discomfort** When people get overly fatigued, nothing looks good to them, particularly their jobs. The dangerous result when members of your staff work several other jobs is that they get physically worn down, which affects their thinking. Their lower state of mind, in turn, has a damaging effect on the work climate in the company. For the same reason, it is counter-productive for management to regularly work 60- or 70-hour weeks. While such hours are common in the industry, and there are occasional times when the additional hours may be required, personal effectiveness goes down rapidly after about 45 hours. It may seem that more hours would equal more productivity, but a burned-out manager lowers the work climate, and thus the productivity, of the entire organization. Besides, people will do what they see you doing. We call this *the shadow of the leader* and it is a powerful way to influence the behavior of others.

3. **Respect/Disrespect** The feeling of respect is a personal issue. Treating your staff with respect means seeing them as intelligent, thinking adults who really want to do the very best they can. When you see people this way, you naturally tend to ask their opinion and advice. You bring them into the planning process. Respect, and the actions that convey it, will

make anyone feel better about themselves, about you, and about your company. On the other hand, when members of your staff feel that you do not respect them as a person, their level of well-being drops and their performance is affected. When your approach to your staff as a whole is interpreted as disrespectful, the climate of the entire operation suffers. Minorities are particularly sensitive to a disrespectful attitude, which is often conveyed by your unconscious actions, choice of words, or voice inflection. Respect does not mean you have to agree or disagree with another person, only that you honestly *consider* what they have to say.

4. **Standards/Rules**   These may seem to be similar concepts but there is an important difference. Rules are cop-based edicts that convey the threat of punishment if they are broken without the promise of reward if they are upheld. Standards, on the other hand, are uniform levels of performance that you can coach people toward. Having clear standards means that someone can be performing below the target and still be productive members of the team as long as they are making progress toward meeting the standard. There can be rewards and encouragement in a world of standards that are impossible in an environment that is all rules. Standards help your staff know what you expect and help them measure how they are doing.

5. **Leadership/Management**   There is a difference between leadership and management. If you call someone a manager, they may try to manage *people*. This is incredibly dangerous. You can manage activities but you have to *lead* people. People do not like to be managed. People love to be led. Management can exist without people—leadership cannot. Leadership is the ability to convey a vision. It is the quality of inspiring people to be more than they thought they were capable of being. Another way to look at it is that leadership is about doing the right thing while management is about doing things right.

6. **Consistency/Inconsistency**   People like to know what they

can count on. For example, I tend to drive a little fast. It occurred to me that if I got a speeding ticket *every* time I exceeded the speed limit, I probably would strictly observe the posted speed and not think too much about it. (I notice I no longer put my hands on hot stoves!) Consistency creates order, which increases the security level of your staff. When the ground rules change in the middle of the game, particularly when it happens without notice, your staff feels more insecure and it is reflected in their behavior. Be sensitive to "standards," either of performance or of enforcement, that change with the supervisor or the supervisor's mood. It happens all the time and the effect on the well-being of your staff is devastating.

7. **Easing/Encumbering**   Do the things you do generally tend to make work easier or more difficult for your staff? The automatic answer is to assume that everything you do has a positive influence because that is your intent when you do it. If you are, in fact, helping make the work easier for your crew, they will feel much better about working with you and look forward to your involvement. In my experience, however, many owners and managers do more harm than good. I see it most often when an absentee owner (or a manager who doesn't listen) tries to "help." Their comments and actions come from a sincere desire to make things better, but the staff sees it as disruptive meddling that usually does more to make things worse than to improve the operation. You can imagine the effect on the well-being of the staff.

8. **Communication/Surprises**   Change is the only constant in business, but how you accomplish that change makes all the difference. Nobody likes to be blind-sided by unexpected changes. To the extent that workers know what to expect and what they can count on from you, they can deal with almost anything. It is when they live in fear of the unexpected that the work climate suffers. Surprise your staff with a change or try to make too many alterations at once and they get insecure. Take the same change and discuss it with people before-

hand, get their input, secure their understanding and (ideally) their concurrence and they will likely feel supportive and positive.

This list could go on and on. I hope you have started to get a sense of what I'm pointing toward. Anything you do that places additional fears and concerns in the minds of your staff lowers their level of well-being. Practices that free their thinking help restore their natural buoyancy and improve their state of mind.

3. Personal Cultures

We are all products of our environment. As we grow up, we learn things from our parents, our peers, the school, the church, and society in general. Events happen, we draw conclusions, and all of these judgments are filed away as lessons. The sum of these experiences (call them values, beliefs, assumptions, etc.) forms our frame of reference for the world. When something comes up, we see it in the context of our life experiences and make a judgment about whether it is good or bad, relevant or irrelevant, a threat or benign.

So what we make of our life experiences determine how we make sense of the world. Looking at life through this framework, each of us says "this is the way it is" and that position is completely validated by our value system.

The problem is that every person has a unique set of experiences and every person's view of the world is an equally valid personal reference. Each person's frame of reference is necessarily different from everyone else's because every person's life experiences (and the conclusions drawn from them) are different. This is true even for identical twins. So while we may still say "this is the way it is," a more valid statement would be "this is the way it looks to me."

Many managers generate a tremendous amount of stress because they try to force their view of the world on their staff. Without understanding that everyone has a unique personal culture, it is easy to think that people who "don't get it" or "refuse to cooperate" by seeing things our way are somehow difficult, stupid, or trouble-makers. In fact, they only have a different frame of reference. Different, not wrong.

We are not going to change the way anyone sees things. We can, however, start to realize that our point of view is only our point of view, not a vision of Ultimate Truth. With this perspective, it may be easier to allow others to hold different opinions without that becoming a personal threat. When you can do this, the result will be a more tolerant work atmosphere in which your staff will be more productive, give better service, and be more likely to stay.

4. Tone of Voice

A fourth insight into dealing with people is that the message you convey is seldom communicated solely by your choice of words.

> The message you deliver is always the feeling behind the tone of voice you use.

Your words are just a vehicle that carries the emphasis, inflections, and feelings that bear the message that others receive. You can probably recall a recent incident in which someone said one thing but conveyed a totally different message by the way they said it. Which message did you believe? This demonstrates the power of tone of voice.

Everybody makes assumptions, forms judgments, and draws conclusions from another's tone of voice. If you have ever watched a foreign language film or been in a country where you did not speak the language, you probably still had a pretty accurate idea of what was happening. You could tell who was happy, sad, confused, angry, or frustrated by the tone of their speech, even if you did not understand all the words.

The typical foodservice manager's day can be hectic. As the pace picks up and the level of stress builds, it is easy to forget the importance of voice tone when dealing with others. Under pressure you can easily snap off a fast answer or react in a way that delivers a message different from the one made up of your words. A gentle, neutral tone fosters an adult relationship between you and your staff which will improve the work climate. In a higher climate, your staff is naturally inclined to provide exceptional service to your guests, feel more involved in their work and stay with you longer.

To help make sure your intonation matches your intention when you are talking with someone, pause before speaking, drop any distracting thoughts, connect with the person you are talking to, and then say what you need to say. It is a process of cleaning up your internal state—a process that is quite natural. When you start becoming aware of your distractions, you will naturally start the process of self-correction. I think you will be surprised and pleased by how clear your communication becomes, how few misunderstandings arise, and how effective you become at human relations.

5. *The Way You Treat Your Staff Is the Way They Will Treat Your Guests*

A final point—and the one you probably didn't want to hear—is that personal example delivers the clearest message of all. You cannot chew your crew out, treat them like errant children, and expect them to go forth to deliver inspired, compassionate service to your guests. What *they* see is what *you* will get. Like it or not, you are the role model. It is just that simple.

If you want your staff to report to work looking sharp, pay attention to your own grooming habits. If you want people to be on time, schedule an arrival time for yourself and be at work when the schedule says you will be. (If you have errands to run, come on time, *then* leave to do your errands.) If you want your crew to be flexible and tolerant with your guests . . . well, you get the picture. Unless you are willing to play as good a game as you talk, you will be in a continual struggle with your staff, one that will eventually wear you down and drive them away.

These are a few insights into people and why they react the way they do. The principles apply to all people regardless of ethnic background or gender. People are just people. Simply understanding the notion offered in this chapter can make you more effective in all your human relationships. When you have your people act together, you are better able to help your staff stay positive and in a state of mind that will cause your good workers to stay.

Effectiveness in this mode requires being more of a teacher and less of a technician—more of a coach and less of a cop. Still, understanding what makes people tick opens the door for lasting results with less effort than you ever believed possible—and without having to wrestle with techniques or a host of petty details. If this sounds interesting, read on.

Chapter Four

Respect the Power of Climate

A healthy climate spawns top performance. People produce more meaningful results in a stress-free, healthy climate than in a high pressure one.

—Robert C. Kausen

Now that you have a few insights into people, let's turn our attention to organizations. Organizations are just a group of individuals and, like individuals, they respond on the basis of the level of thinking of the people in them. What we called state of mind in individuals we call climate in an organization. Another way to look at climate is to think of it as the level of mental health in the organization.

The more positive the work climate in a company, the more positive, service-oriented, efficient, and effective the organization will be. When it comes to the issues of turnover and teamwork, the entire key lies in the climate.

> Turnover is a natural consequence of a low climate.
> Teamwork is a natural consequence of a high climate.

The work climate of the company ultimately determines the behavior that the members of the group are likely to exhibit. Here is

47

how human relations consultant Robert Kausen, puts this notion into perspective:

> *While the understanding about human functioning will vary widely among employees, psychological reaction to the human relations climate is predictable and consistent. Peak performance is possible only without distracting thoughts. The single greatest distraction for people is insecure (unhealthy) thinking. Only people with unusually high inner security (self-esteem) can remain unaffected by the ravages of an insecure climate. The rest either play the game (politics, indecisiveness, non-responsibility) or leave.*

Despite what you may have been led to believe, people will actually be more productive in a stress-free, supportive environment than they will in a high pressure climate. The actions outlined in the preceding chapter will help calm an anxious worker. People naturally feel more secure and perform better in a supportive work climate.

People do not want to live in a state of turmoil; they just see no other option. When you understand what is happening, you can use these symptoms as indicators of the level of insecurity in the environment. Just wanting an environment that is safe and secure goes a long way toward calming storms. Treating people with respect and consideration is a major step in building a healthy climate.

> The climate of an organization starts at the top.

The good news and the bad news is that the climate always reflects the person in charge. When the boss has a bad day, *everybody* will tend to be a little off track and slightly less effective. The most potent thing you bring to the job is your own mental health.

Because few operators are fully aware of the importance of the atmosphere they create, many unwittingly foster an environment that almost guarantees that their staff will not be able to reach maximum productivity or have a pleasant work experience. If your business has a depressing environment, it affects the mood of your staff and starts to bring them down. In a lower mood, minor events take on more significance. Your workers are less trusting of others and more inclined to find fault and complain. They are harder to please and more likely to leave.

If workers do not feel that their supervisors are looking out for their best interests, then the staff members will spend time looking out for themselves. When that happens, you are likely to see any or all of these symptoms of insecure thinking:

Looking out for Number One. Teamwork and cooperation cannot exist in a climate where people are worried about their own safety and security. This insecurity can also take the form of empire building or craving and hoarding information.

Malicious compliance. You may not be familiar with the term, but I am sure you are familiar with the behavior. Malicious compliance is when your staff does *exactly* what you tell them to do (and *not one thing more*) and do it *exactly* the way you tell them to, even if they know their behavior will not accomplish the results you are trying to get.

Increased sickness and absenteeism. People won't come to work if they don't want to. I'm sure you can find times in your own career when you became disenchanted with a job and called in sick under circumstances that previously would not have kept you from work.

Accidents and poor safety record. When people feel insecure, they are easily preoccupied or distracted. When people would have on-the-job accidents in places where I have worked in the past, it was usually not because they did not know what they should have done but because they got distracted and didn't do it.

Low morale. Suspicion, lack of trust, whining, and complaining are sure signals that the climate has dropped. If the climate stays low, there is no way you can improve morale because *everything* looks like a problem to people. When the work climate improves, the petty sniping will just go away on its own. In a more positive environment, a tricky situation is just another thing to handle, not a personal threat.

Increased union pressure. Unions feed on businesses with low climates. When your staff feels insecure, the union's pitch can seem like a life raft in rough seas. Without dissatisfaction on the job, a union has no product to sell.

When you notice symptoms that the climate has slipped a bit, don't panic. Just take it as a wake-up call—a message that you have not been paying proper attention to the care and feeding of your business environment. When I would encounter whining and complaining at the OTC, it was just a signal that I had been spending too much time in the office. I would pay more attention to the dining room staff and help the kitchen crew get what they needed. As the level came up again, the whining went away on its own.

> To change work performance, change the work
> environment.

A lasting solution to most operating issues involves a change in behavior, and the simplest way to change behavior is to change the work environment. When the work environment changes, thinking changes, and most problems will resolve themselves without much further attention.

Understanding the relationship between actions and level of thinking, you start to see that there are not bad people, only good people who get stuck in unproductive thinking. Now some people can stay stuck in insecure thinking for a long time, but that does not make them inherently bad people. If you have ever done anything really stupid in your life (and who hasn't?) then you know what can happen when good people get stuck. Give folks a little slack.

A compassionate leader understands that staff members are always doing exactly what makes sense to them, given their state of mind at the moment and their conditioned thinking. Negative attitudes and poor performance are just innocent conduct, not willful treachery.

When you fully respect the power of climate, foodservice management becomes a much easier, much more enjoyable game to play.

Rather than cluttering your head with techniques, all you need to do is understand what affects the climate. Then you just implement more of the things that foster goodwill and trust and eliminate those practices that contribute to fear and insecurity.

AN ADDICTION TO EMERGENCIES

Crisis management is seductive because it provides an excuse to drop the distracting games and just do the job. Companies often get trapped in the crisis cycle out of habit because they do not realize that it is possible to build a healthy climate where crises seldom appear. My experience of managing the foodservice operation at the Olympic Training Center convinced me that easily 80 percent of the problems that I used to pride myself on being able to solve never even showed up! Well, I suppose they might have appeared; it's just that nobody noticed. If you have a crisis and it seems like just another thing to handle, was it a crisis or not?

MAINTAINING A POSITIVE CLIMATE

What are the management qualities that contribute to creating and maintaining a supportive climate? My experience has led me to consider the following qualities among those that are most essential:

1. **Maintain a benefit-of-a-doubt stance**   This quality merely acknowledges that there is always more information than you have in your possession and commits you to getting all the facts before you act. For example, if Karen has been late three times in the past and she's late again today, it would be easy to draw a hasty conclusion about Karen. However, today may be the day her child was hit by a car and she's had other priorities to attend to. This does not necessarily mean that you will buy her story, just that you want to hear her side of the issue before you make up your mind. Remember that mistrust only begets mistrust.

2. **Serve your staff** When I think of serving my staff, the picture that always comes to mind is of the Canadian sport of curling. If you've never seen it, I would describe it as being something like shuffleboard on ice. One member of the team gives a heavy stone a push down the ice toward a target. Two other team members move along ahead of the stone, sweeping the ice with brooms. The job of the sweepers is to make the ice slicker or slower as needed and to eliminate anything that might snag the stone, impede its progress, or throw it off course.

   The analogy closely parallels the new model of management. In the traditional style of foodservice management, the manager's job is to push the stone through any obstacles that lie in its path. The new model recognizes that the business has its own momentum and the proper focus of management should be to keep that energy flowing unimpeded rather than trying to force the flow.

3. **Value and respect your staff** On one level, think of what it would be like if everybody walked out in the middle of the dinner rush. On an entirely different level, when you allow yourself to connect with your staff as human beings, you will be moved by their innocence and heroism. I think it is heroic for a single mother to try to raise three children while working as a waitress. I think it is heroic to be sixteen—it is a lot harder job now than it was when we did it! When you allow yourself this human connection, you will start treating people well because you will see that they deserve the best level of care you can muster.

4. **Value a free and clear mind** Start to realize that the most potent thing you bring to the job is your own mental health. Remember that the climate of the organization always starts at the top. The reason you cannot regularly work 60 or more hours a week is that your mind gets scrambled, your own level of well-being drops, and the productivity of the entire organization suffers.

5. **Support your staff** In the long term, the only way our or-

ganizations can succeed is if the people who comprise these organizations succeed. When we select people to become part of our staff, it must represent a commitment on the part of the company (supported by our deeds) to do everything possible to encourage and support their development, both personally and professionally. If you are not comfortable making that level of commitment to an individual, you should not bring that person on board.

Experience and maturity have long been generally accepted qualifications for effective foodservice management and I do not mean to minimize their importance. However, in my experience, managers of any age who approach their jobs like coaches instead of cops and focus on developing and maintaining a supportive work climate will achieve results that most "experienced" managers can only dream about.

So in the end, the path from turnover to teamwork is simply a matter of creating and maintaining a nurturing work environment. In that type of climate, insecurity diminishes and people are free to do their jobs. In the chapters that follow, we will explore some specific programs that will help enlightened management establish and preserve this sort of climate. Still, it is important to understand that reducing turnover and improving teamwork are a natural result of a higher climate and are not brought about by the support programs themselves.

Part Three

Building the Bridge

Chapter Five

Get a Good Start

Most new workers who fail do so because they didn't get enough information from management right at the start.
—National Restaurant Association

It is perhaps the eternal cliché that you don't get a second chance for a first impression. Still, that is precisely the role that orientation plays in your overall staff retention program. Just as your professional success depends on meeting (and exceeding!) your guests' expectations, success with your staff is also built on expectations. Orientation is your chance to meet and exceed the expectations of your new staff members, share your values and vision, and help them bond with the company. If you lose this opportunity at the beginning of your professional relationship, you can never effectively regain it.

The two essential elements of a good start on the job are a strong orientation and an effective adjustment period. Since orientation is the first step on the job, let's start there.

ORIENTATION

1. Why

The foodservice business can be hectic and it is often hard to find time to do the little things. You also know that if you don't take care of the details you won't be in business long. We opened this book with a discussion of what turnover costs and you were probably reminded again this month that turnover carries a real price in terms of lost productivity, customer complaints, time, and dollars.

While it is certainly possible to do a better job of selecting higher-quality candidates the first time around, at best you get only a promissory note that the person chosen will be a future star. In the final analysis effective workers are actually created—by you. You know how it feels to be a stranger in a strange place. That's how it feels to most workers the first day on the job. It can be scary. But the fear comes simply because there are a few things the new staff member does not know.

When you start to understand how insecurity affects a person's thinking and behavior, you will also understand the need to build a strong bridge over this initial period of introduction to the company.

2. When

Orientation should be completed before a new worker ever steps onto the floor to start work or training. If you rush someone onto the job and promise that you will handle their orientation later (when you have a chance), several things may happen: First, you will never get around to the orientation because your life is already a series of crises and there are certain to be more. Second, the new worker will be tossed to the sharks without the support needed to be successful. This increases the likelihood that the worker will make mistakes, develop bad habits or feel like a failure, any of which can trigger the worker's decision not to stay with your company. To be fair, a third possibility is that you may actually see to it that the orientation is done, but you know the odds of that happening are slim.

3. Who

Because the first step is so important, orientation should be conducted by the most senior person possible. McGuffey's, an extremely successful multi-unit operator in the Southeast takes orientation so seriously that they always have the program conducted by one of the company's owners. In their experience, when someone of lesser authority chairs the session, new workers do not get the same perspective of the culture and vision that are key to the company's success nor do they feel quite as important.

Larger organizations may already have a training manager who specializes in conducting new staff orientation. Like anything else, orientation skills are sharpened by repeated practice. I suggest that you will benefit more by having fewer experienced people conducting orientations more often than simply by tossing the task to whoever is free at the moment.

4. Where

Orientations should be conducted in an area that is private and quiet. The goal is to have an environment where the trainer and the new staff members can get to understand each other and where the new workers can comfortably ask questions and concentrate on the content and spirit of the orientation. This means that the person conducting the orientation should not be pulled away from the task to take care of the needs of guests, telephone calls, or other operational demands.

If you cannot find a location on the premises that meets the necessary criteria for a successful orientation, consider holding the session away from the property. Even if you have to hold orientation over coffee in a competitor's operation or pay for a meeting room, the inconvenience or expense is worth it. Orientation is an investment that will help you get maximum value from your most precious assets, your staff.

5. What

The following checklist covers the essential elements that should be part of an effective staff orientation program. It was adapted from material developed by the National Restaurant Association (reprinted with permission). Use it as a guide to help make sure that every important item is covered during the orientation so that each

new member of your staff gets the right start. It will also help you
organize everything you and the new worker should talk about on
the first day. Items marked with an asterisk (*) suggest there could
be a state or federal law governing your policy in this area. If you are
unsure, check with your state restaurant association, or call the National Restaurant Association for clarification.

Purpose of Orientation

❏ *To introduce you to our establishment*
❏ *To get help you fit in and work well here*
❏ *To explain our policies and goals*
❏ *To answer all your questions*
❏ *To explain how you will be trained and what happens next*

What We Are All About

❏ *History of the company*
　　❏ *How we came to be—when, where and why*
　　❏ *Who owns the company*
　　❏ *If a franchise, a short history of the parent company*
　　❏ *What's special about us—stories connected with us, awards
　　　received, famous guests*

Expectations

❏ *What we expect from you*
　　❏ *a day's work for a day's pay*
　　❏ *your commitment to good service and fine food quality*
　　❏ *concern for your co-workers and cooperation with our team*
❏ *What you can expect from us*
　　❏ *proper training, so you know how to do your job*
　　❏ *good working conditions*
　　❏ *reasonable compensation for your efforts*
　　❏ *recognition and reward for a job well done*
　　❏ *respect and constant communication from management*

Organizational Structure

❏ *Chart of departments and supervisory levels*
❏ *Where you fit in the organization*
❏ *Who you report to*
❏ *Who reports to you*

Payroll Policies

❏ *How often payday is (length of pay periods)*
❏ *When you can expect your first paycheck*
❏ *How you will get your check*
❏ *Who to see if you have questions about it*
❏ *Information needed for withholding: SSN, address, marital status, etc.*
❏ **What deductions will be made*
❏ **Eligibility for overtime and how it is calculated*
❏ **Tip reporting requirements and procedures*
❏ **Tip credit to be taken*
❏ *Policy on lost paychecks*
❏ *Policy on early issuance of paychecks*
❏ *Policy on advances or loans against pay*

Work Schedules

❏ *Hours of operation*
❏ *When and how your schedule is determined*
❏ *What your initial schedule will be*
❏ *How—and if—changes in the schedule can be made*
❏ *Who to see about changes*
❏ **Timekeeping procedures (time clock, time cards, etc.)*
❏ *Policy on absenteeism*
❏ *Policy on reporting late*
❏ *How and when to report in if you are ill or expect to be late*

Breaks and Meals

- ❑ *When break times are scheduled
- ❑ *How many and how long
- ❑ *How to record break time
- ❑ *Whether breaks and meals are paid or unpaid time
- ❑ *How meal breaks are scheduled
- ❑ *How much time is allowed for meals and when
- ❑ *Whether or not you can leave the premises
- ❑ *Policy for interrupting breaks or meals because of customer need
- ❑ *Where to take breaks and meals
- ❑ *How much meals are (% of cost? free?)
- ❑ *How to record them (on guest check? check on time card?)
- ❑ What may or may not be eaten
- ❑ Policy on coffee, soft drinks, etc.

Uniforms/Dress Code

- ❑ Grooming standards
- ❑ Hair clean, appropriate hairdo, proper covering
- ❑ *Length of hair
- ❑ *Facial hair rules
- ❑ Basic cleanliness, especially hand-washing
- ❑ Description of the uniform or dress required for your job
- ❑ Where to get the uniform
- ❑ *Who pays for it and how
- ❑ *If a deposit is required
- ❑ *How the uniform is to be maintained
- ❑ When you are expected to have your uniform; what happens if you don't have it
- ❑ What happens to the uniform when you leave (buy back?)
- ❑ Policy on types of shoes, sandals, etc.
- ❑ Policy on socks and hose
- ❑ Policy on make-up and jewelry

For Tipped Employees

❑ *Form or procedure for recording tips
❑ *How often tips will be reported
❑ *How credit card charges are handled*
❑ *When tip reports must be turned in to assure paycheck*
❑ *How deductions will be made on reported tips (state and federal withholding, SS, etc.)*

Salary and Performance Review

❑ *If there is an adjustment period, how long it is and what is expected*
❑ *How often you will be reviewed*
❑ *When you will be reviewed*
❑ *Who will review you*
❑ *What the criteria for review are*
❑ *How you will be notified of raises*
❑ *When raises will become effective*

Miscellaneous Whats and Wheres

❑ *Layout of the establishment—where things are (walk-through)*
❑ *Where to enter and leave the building*
❑ *Where to park, where not to park*
❑ *Where to put your personal belongings (management's responsibility for them?)*
❑ *Where the staff restrooms are*

Grounds for Dismissal

❑ *Number of warnings before termination*
❑ *Time allowed for corrections*
❑ *Conduct that can result in termination*
    ❑ *continued violation of policies*
    ❑ *insubordination*

❑ *frequent tardiness and/or absenteeism*
❑ *lack of cooperation with fellow staff members*
❑ *improper respect for our guests*
❑ *Conduct that can mean immediate dismissal*
  ❑ *drunkenness*
  ❑ *drug use*
  ❑ *abusiveness toward a guest or co-worker*
  ❑ *theft*

Quitting/Termination

❑ *How to give notice if you are quitting*
❑ *How much notice is expected*
❑ **When and how you will receive your final check*
❑ *If terminated, if there is severance pay (and under what conditions)*

Policies (if any) We Have About

❑ *Before and after work hours conduct on premises*
❑ *Moonlighting*
❑ *Hiring of relatives of employees*
❑ *Profanity*
❑ *Personal phone calls and/or visitors*

Promotions

❑ *If management does promote from within*
❑ *How you can apply*
❑ *What criteria other than current job performance will be considered for the promotion*
❑ *If passed over, how you will be notified of why and what to do to improve*

Breakage and Errors

❑ **Whether you will be held responsible for careless breakage or errors on guest checks*

❑ *conditions for determining whether you will be charged*
❑ *how much will be charged*
❑ *how staff will pay (payroll deduction? cash transaction?)*

Sanitation

❑ *Importance of good sanitation*
❑ *How you will learn our standards*
❑ *Importance of frequent hand-washing*
❑ *Policy on smoking*

Emergency Procedures

❑ *How and when to report accidents on the job*
❑ *What to do in case of fire*
❑ *What to do in case of power failure*
❑ *What to do in case of bad weather (storm, tornado, blizzard, hurricane, whatever fits)*
❑ *Where the first aid kit is and who has access to it*
❑ *Injured guest (911, Heimlich Maneuver, etc.)*

Holidays

❑ *Which holidays we are open and which ones we are closed*
❑ *How the work schedules are determined for those days*
❑ *If any special pay or consideration is given for working those days*

Loss Prevention

❑ *How you can help (portion control, waste prevention, proper inventory control, etc.)*
❑ *Policy on theft*
❑ *Policy on bonding*
❑ *Policy on polygraph tests*

Vacations

❑ *Who is eligible for vacation pay (FT? PT?)*

❑ *How long you must work here to be eligible*

❑ *Whether you must take vacation, can get paid for it instead, or can accumulate it*

❑ *How much vacation pay you will get*

❑ **How vacation pay is calculated for tipped workers*

❑ *How much in advance vacations must be scheduled*

❑ *Who gets first priority for dates or times of the year*

❑ *Who to see about scheduling vacation time*

Sick Leave

❑ *Who is eligible for sick leave*

❑ *How long you must work here to be eligible*

❑ *Whether you can accumulate it, or get extra pay for unused days*

❑ *How much sick leave, per month, per year, etc.*

❑ *Whether a doctor's statement is required after a prolonged illness*

Insurance

❑ *What kind of insurance is offered: health, major medical, life, disability, dental*

❑ *When and how to become eligible*

❑ *Whether your family will be covered as well*

❑ *How much you and the company each pay*

❑ *How your share will be taken (payroll deduction? which paycheck? each month?)*

❑ *When and how you will receive more details about the program(s)*

Other Benefits

❑ *What other benefits we offer*
  ❑ *pension or profit-sharing plan?*
  ❑ *bonus system?*
  ❑ *discounts for staff members' families or parties?*
  ❑ *holiday bonus and/or party?*
  ❑ *educational assistance?*

❑ *credit union?*
❑ *What it takes to become eligible*
❑ *How each works and how much participants receive*
❑ *Who to see to get more information*

What happens now?

❑ *Description of the job*
❑ *How you will be trained*
❑ *Who will do the training*
❑ *How long it will take*

Remember that this checklist is just the beginning of a total communication commitment to each new member of your staff. There are undoubtedly items that you will want to add to the list (the menu, operating policies peculiar to your operation, corporate philosophy, and so forth). Orientation will be most effective when it is followed up by planned staff training and ongoing staff communication.

ADJUSTMENT PERIOD

Everybody needs a little time to get comfortable with a new job and their new co-workers. Most typically, this takes the form of a 90-day probationary period. The idea is good, but I always found the reality of it to be difficult. See if these problems sound familiar:

1. **A probation period does not accomplish much.** Without a clear requirement for what must be accomplished during the probation period, it becomes little more than a limbo-like waiting period.

2. **Decisions are often made without proper consideration.** Ninety days has a way of flying past. When the probation period is "suddenly" over, management is faced with a go/no go decision with no real criteria for the choice other than

whether or not the worker made any serious mistakes since they started work.

3. **It is unfair.**   A straight 90-day probation for all workers means that you don't have as much time to look at part-timers as you do to look at full-timers. Since the reality of probation periods is that they are primarily a chance to see whether the new worker makes any major mistakes, the structure actually works against full-timers because they have more opportunity to slip.

4. **Probation is a "cop" term.**   To make the leap between being a cop and being a coach, you must eliminate any terms that have an unwanted connotation. Probation does not exactly sound supportive.

Confirmation Period

When I was developing the operating policies for my management company, Prototype Restaurants, I wanted to find a better answer than a standard 90-day probation period. Consistent with the idea of never wasting time solving a problem you can eliminate, my answer to the problems described above was what I called a confirmation period. I arrived at the term because what I wanted was really an adjustment period during which both the company and the new staff member would confirm that they had made a good decision and that continued on-the-job success was likely.

Figure 5-1 is a copy of the details of the confirmation period from the Prototype Restaurants Staff Manual. Most of it is self-explanatory, but there are a few twists that are worth some clarification:

Fixed duration.   There is a defined length of the confirmation period. It lasts a minimum of 160 hours but no longer than 320 hours. This means that a full-time worker could get on regular staff in as little as a month. It also requires that if all the requirements of the confirmation period have not been met after 320 hours on the job, the worker *must* be dismissed. This provision helps ensure that only those workers who apply themselves seriously to the company's standards will become part of the regular staff.

Equal treatment. The confirmation period is based solely on hours worked, so the company has the same amount of time to look at full-timers and part-timers. It also means that both full-time and part-time staff have the same amount of time to decide if they want to make a commitment to your organization.

Contingency wage. Since most workers expect a raise when their probation is up anyway, it is built into the system. The contingency wage is essentially a training wage. Upon successfully completing the confirmation period, the new worker will receive a raise to bring them up to the starting wage for their position (or perhaps higher if their performance was exceptional).

Tests. In order to complete the confirmation period, the new worker must show proficiency in the areas of safety, sanitation, dish machine operation and cleaning. The idea is to help demystify these functions, underscore the importance of all these areas to the success of the restaurant, and give everyone on staff—managers and hourly workers alike—a basic proficiency.

Endorsements. Successful completion of the confirmation period requires that both the coaches (managers) and co-workers agree that they support bringing the new worker into the company. The impact of this requirement on team-building is obvious.

Incentive. The new worker has control over the length of time the contingency period lasts. In effect, they can give themselves a raise and start to accrue benefits in half the time by applying themselves and completing the requirements of the confirmation period quickly.

Habit development. An interesting condition of the confirmation period is that there be no unexcused absences or disciplinary action in the 160 hours immediately preceding confirmation. This means that every time new workers make an error in judgment, they must put in at least another 160 hours before they are eligible for regular staff status. This also means that if new workers make an error in judgment after 160 hours on the job, they must be dismissed because they will not be able to fulfill this requirement of confirmation before their 320 hour maximum, and you might just as well drop them.

CONFIRMATION PERIOD

EFFECTIVE DATE:

A newly hired staff member will have a period of adjustment to their job, the restaurant and the company's policies and procedures. The confirmation period will extend for at least 160 hours worked but not more than 320 hours worked. During the confirmation period, there will be continuing communication between the individual and the coach about training requirements and performance expectations of the job.

If the staff member successfully completes the confirmation period, they will be performing effectively and will know the company's policies and procedures.

CONTINGENT WAGE

Contingent staff will receive the contingency wage for their position. Upon acceptance as regular staff, their wage will change to the minimum of the salary range for their position. The coach can authorize a higher starting rate when the individual has shown exceptional performance during the confirmation period. In any case, the coach cannot authorize a starting wage above the first percentile of the salary range without prior approval of the Managing Director.

CHANGE OF STATUS

Anytime after 160 hours worked, the company may accept a contingent staff member on the regular staff. The following must have occurred:

1. The individual has successfully passed tests on sanitation practices, safety procedures, dish machine operation and cleaning.
2. The individual has the recommendation of the coaches.

Figure 5-1　Details of the Confirmation Period (from the Prototype Restaurants Human Resources Manual)

3. The individual has a vote of confidence from their co-workers.
4. The individual has received a satisfactory performance appraisal.
5. The individual has no unexcused absences or disciplinary action in the preceding 160 hours worked.

The company may, at will, dismiss contingent staff at any time during the confirmation period without prior notice. If any of the above conditions has not been met at the end of 320 hours worked (or cannot be met within 320 hours worked), the individual must be discharged.

Note: For an explanation of terms in the Prototype manuals, refer to the Glossary on p. 175.

Figure 5-1 *(continued)*

Drop dead date. If the requirements of the confirmation period have not (or cannot) be met within 320 hours, the worker *must* be terminated. This requirement ensures that all regular staff members have shown the same professional competence and taken an active interest in their own success.

I should emphasize that the confirmation period is the time when both the company and the new staff member can clearly demonstrate their commitment to making the relationship successful. Every new worker is ultimately responsible for their own success, but the actions of the coaches should demonstrate their belief in the competence of the new hire.

Toward this end, some companies assign every new worker a buddy or a mentor. The mentor's job is to help the new worker adjust, answer questions, interpret events, and in general be a resource for the new person's success with the company. Ideally, the mentor would be a peer of the contingent (newly hired) worker rather than a supervisor or a person who would evaluate the person's performance during the confirmation period.

Chapter Six

Put It in Writing

[Following orientation] the next logical step is a full employee policy manual—a "staff handbook" that puts in writing all of the items covered orally . . . plus all the other items that are important to you, your staff and your business. It is an important next step and highly recommended.

—National Restaurant Association

At the outset, I should say that I am not an unqualified fan of manuals. Too many operators have tried to control their operations by putting everything in writing and then expecting that their staffs would read, understand, and follow the gospel. I question how well this approach works. For example, the operating manual for one major fast food chain is over five inches thick! In the real world, how many people (other than the author) do you suspect are really going to become intimate with almost half a foot of paper? On the other hand, the discipline of committing your thoughts to writing forces you to drop any fuzzy thinking and get very clear about how you want things in your company to work.

Manuals definitely serve a purpose in modern foodservice operations, but not all manuals are helpful. Let me share a few ideas on foodservice manuals:

Staff Manual. The staff manual contains all the basic information about the company that every member of the staff needs to be a functioning part of the company culture. Much of it is information covered verbally in the staff orientation session, along with a summary of other helpful information the new worker will want to know. It is written in an informal, conversational style to make it easier and more interesting to read. A staff manual is an essential part of a retention program.

Human Resources Manual. The HR manual details the company's policies relating to people. It is important for several reasons: First of all, it is information that all your staff will want to know anyway and failure to have the answers will lower the working climate. Second, you must comply with a tangle of state and federal laws that govern your personnel policies. The HR manual helps ensure that you have considered and devised an approach to all of them. Without this roadmap, you run the risk of innocently violating one or more labor statutes, with potentially serious consequences. You really need an HR manual to produce even a meaningful staff manual, so add this one to your list.

Policy Manual. I can also make a case for a simple policy manual—containing no more than ten major points—to keep everyone in the operation moving in roughly the same philosophical direction. For the sake of simplicity, these points could easily be made part of the staff manual.

Procedure Manual. I am not a fan of procedure manuals—those detailed "do-it-this-way" manuals (as opposed to a "here's-the-way-it-works" book explaining, for example, the computerized POS system). My concern is that typical procedure manuals can easily stifle creativity and actually make your professional life more complicated. The problem is that they typically spell out a set of specific activities that management wants the staff to follow. In my experience, the key to productivity is to define the results you seek rather than the activities involved. When you define only the results, you leave the people free to interpret their jobs in a way that works for them. This makes coaching easier and also increases workers' involvement with their jobs and their identification with the company, all of which contribute to a higher retention rate while making the job of management easier and more pleasant.

PRODUCING MANUALS

The difficulty for most operators is finding time to write manuals. The daily demands of a foodservice operation are considerable and it is hard to fix the car while you are driving it! Just as an oyster needs a grain of sand to start making a pearl, often all it takes is a starting point to get a set of manuals started. One idea is to follow the orientation checklist in Chapter 5. Another approach is to adapt someone else's manuals to meet your own needs.

To help you start the process, the section that follows gives you the contents of the staff and human resources manuals for Prototype Restaurants. Excerpts from the manuals are included in several other chapters, and Figures 6-1 through 6-3 in this chapter give you the flavor of the text. The excerpts and the list of contents are not intended as the definitive solution to what you need in your manuals. They only provide a suggestion as to what could be included.

Even with an outline, the process of writing manuals is never easy. It took nearly six months to write my manuals . . . and I wasn't trying to operate a restaurant at the same time! The Law of Creative Laziness[1] suggests that you don't try to write manuals from scratch if you can get copies of other operators' manuals and revise them to meet your own requirements. It is always easier to edit than to create. See the "Resources for Retention" section for suggestions on where to obtain model manuals.

Staff Manual

The Prototype Restaurants staff manual contains the following sections:

SECTION 1—BACKGROUND
SM–101   About the Company
SM–102   Corporate Goals
SM–103   The Name of the Game

SM–104   Service Guarantee
SM–105   Expectations
         (see Figure 6-1)
SM–106   Basic Guideline

[1]Never do any more work than is necessary to achieve the results you want.

EXPECTATIONS

EFFECTIVE DATE: _____

The foodservice industry depends on expectations. To be successful, a restaurant must meet and exceed the guests' expectations. Likewise, PROTOTYPE RESTAURANTS has expectations of you. Your success also requires that you meet or exceed those expectations.

WHAT WE EXPECT FROM YOU . . .
Proper Use of Time
We expect you to be on time, all the time. We expect you to leave and return from your breaks on time. We expect you to complete your shift every day. We expect you to set appropriate priorities in doing your daily tasks and to meet our deadlines every time.

Proper Sanitation and Safety Practices
We expect you to know and follow proper sanitation practices. We expect you to work accident-free. We expect you to recognize and report potential sanitation and safety hazards promptly.

Professional Appearance and Attitude
We expect you to look sharp. We expect you to be serious about excellence in your work.

Attractive, Clean and Neat Work Areas
We expect your work areas to reflect your commitment to excellence and professionalism.

Job Knowledge and Skill Development
We expect you to know your job and be good at it. We also expect you to show a professional curiosity. We expect a continuing desire to increase your knowledge and improve your

Figure 6–1   Section on Expectations
(from the Prototype Restaurants Staff Manual)

skills. We expect your work will always bring a positive response from our guests.

Proper Working Attitudes

We expect you to be flexible with unexpected changes. We expect a "no problem" approach to your work. We expect a genuine desire to find solutions rather than to dwell on problems. We expect you to know what to do . . . and we expect you to do it.

Contribution to Company Goals

We expect you to advance our company goals in everything you do here. We expect you to be an active member of the company and to make suggestions for improvements in the operation.

Proper Handling of Food Items

We expect you to handle food properly. This means proper receiving. It means prompt and proper storage. It means appropriate handling during preparation. It means proper temperatures and proper handling of leftovers. It also means not concealing defective products. It means following the right recipes and producing only items that meet our specifications and standards.

Fast, Accurate and Complete Work

We expect you to develop "good hands." We expect you to work quickly, accurately and safely. We expect you to help your co-workers do the same.

Teamwork

We expect you to make your co-workers look good. We expect you to avoid negative humor (getting a laugh by putting someone else down). We expect you to help each other succeed in achieving company and personal goals. We expect you to fill in where needed to assure the smooth operation of the dining room and kitchen. We expect you to support the restaurant, the company and the staff who make it happen. We expect you to be a player.

Figure 6-1   *(continued)*

It is also fair that you should have some expectations of the company.

WHAT YOU CAN EXPECT FROM US . . .

Consistency

We will not change the rules in the middle of the game without notice and discussion. We will conduct ourselves the way we'd like you to conduct yourselves. We will do what we say we will do. If we make a mistake, we will apologize for it and move on. You can count on us.

Proper Training

We can never do as much training as we'd like. However, we'll do everything we can to help you advance your skills and improve your skills. Much of the training you'll receive will be done on the job from your coaches and co-workers. As we find video training tapes that have relevance to our work, we'll share those with you. Trade magazines will be available for your review. We'll provide access to educational seminars and the chance to move among our restaurants to broaden your work experience. In short, we will make a real effort to help you succeed here.

Good Working Conditions

We'll treat you well. You'll have a secure, clean place to store your personal items. We will maintain a clean and well-run operation to work in. Your coaches will take a real interest in your success and well-being.

Reasonable Pay for Your Efforts

We'll regularly compare our pay scales to current wages in the area to assure we offer competitive pay. Our benefit package is exceptional for the industry and adds considerable additional value to your regular pay.

A Chance to Share in the Wealth

We have a profit-sharing bonus plan where you can share in

Figure 6-1 *(continued)*

the success of the restaurant. Your coach will give you the specifics on what it takes to participate.

Recognition and Reward

We base pay raises on your performance and contribution to our financial success. The better job you do, the more likely that your check will reflect your performance.

Respect and Communication

We can prosper only if you succeed. Perhaps more than most places you've worked, we give you the latitude to interpret your job in a way that works for you. All we ask is that you achieve the results we want. What we accomplish is the direct result of your efforts and talent. We will keep you informed about everything you need to do your job better. We will ask for your suggestions and listen to your concerns. If you have any problems, you'll find us attentive. The coaching staff is always available to listen and help resolve any issues that interfere with your peace of mind.

Figure 6-1 *(continued)*

Human Resources Manual

The Prototype Restaurants human resources manual contains the following sections:

TELEPHONES

EFFECTIVE DATE: September 1, 1991

TELEPHONE ETIQUETTE

The telephone is one of the major methods of communication for the company and its restaurants. Callers get their impressions from the voice and manner of the person who answers the telephone. The first impression either invites them to come or tells them to stay home. Staff should build the company's reputation by *always* answering the telephone using these guidelines:

1. Answer the phone by the third ring.
2. Smile before picking up the telephone.
3. Thank the person for calling.
4. Identify the operation and give your name.
5. Be tactful in asking the caller questions.
6. Be helpful to the caller.
7. Be discreet in giving out information.
8. Keep a pad and pencil handy and take complete messages.

TELEPHONE KNOWLEDGE

Every staff member should have the following information before answering the telephone:

1. The operating hours of the restaurant.
2. The daily specials.
3. Directions on how to get to the restaurant from principal parts of the market area.
4. Description of the restaurant's menu style and price levels.

Figure 6–2   Section on Telephones
(from the Prototype Restaurants Human Resources Manual)

TELEPHONES ARE FOR BUSINESS

Company telephones are for the conduct of company business. Therefore, staff should not use the telephones to make or receive personal phone calls during their work day except during breaks. Personal calls must be kept to a minimum. Staff members may make or receive emergency telephone calls as dictated by the emergency.

Figure 6-2 *(continued)*

TAX-SHELTERED SAVINGS ACCOUNT

EFFECTIVE DATE:

PROTOTYPE provides a 401(k) tax-sheltered savings (TSS) program for its staff in the interest of helping staff members prepare financially for retirement.

ELIGIBILITY

All regular staff are eligible for participation in the TSS. Contingent and temporary staff are not eligible to participate in the TSS.

CONTRIBUTIONS

PROTOTYPE will pay bonuses, unused benefits contributions and tuition support to the staff member's TSS. Additionally, the individual may choose to deposit a portion of their paycheck to their TSS.

ADMINISTRATIVE RESPONSIBILITY

The Business Manager is responsible for coordinating the requirements of the TSS.

TAX CONSIDERATIONS

Under the law, funds placed in the TSS are not subject to federal or state taxes until the account holder withdraws them. There may also be penalties for withdrawal under certain conditions. Staff members are responsible for such taxes and penalties, if any, and should seek counsel from a tax professional.

Figure 6–3   Section on Tax-Sheltered Savings Account (from the Prototype Restaurants Human Resources Manual)

Chapter Seven

Eliminate Inequities

Fairness, justice, or whatever you call it—it's essential and most companies don't have it.

—Robert Townsend

When attempting to establish equity in your company, it helps to realize that poverty is relative—whoever has the least tends to feel oppressed, no matter how much they have. This is why a professional athlete making $4 million a year feels the need to whine and complain when a peer gets a contract for $4.1 million! On the job, if workers feel that other comparable individuals or groups have a better deal than they do, it makes them feel less secure regardless of how much they are getting. They can even feel this way if the gap between the compensation package for staff and management seems too wide.

The feeling of having less than one's peers has a serious impact on most workers' sense of personal well-being. When an entire group is affected, inequity can be a major factor in a lowered work climate.

In foodservice, inequity most typically appears in the form of differing benefit packages for full-time versus part-time workers. Since many operations rely heavily on part-time workers and because the feeling of inequity can be so damaging to morale, the challenge is how to level the playing field, be able to treat all workers the same, and still keep control of costs.

DISAPPEARING THE PROBLEM[1]

My solution to this dilemma is to base all benefits, monetary and non-monetary, strictly on hours worked. Because they are working more hours, full-time workers will accrue benefits faster than part-timers, but all workers build up benefits at exactly the same pace.

Rather than talk in the abstract, let's examine the various elements of the Prototype Restaurants benefit plan to illustrate how this concept would look in practice.

BENEFITS CONTRIBUTION

For the sake of illustration, assume that you are willing to pay full health insurance costs for your staff. Worker A is a 20-year-old single male whose premium is $100 per month. Worker B is a married woman with a family whose insurance costs $400 per month. Worker C is a married man whose wife works for a local corporation, is covered under her insurance plan and does not need coverage from your company.

If you pay the full premiums for A and B but not C, you have two problems. Worker A is disgruntled because he sees a peer essentially making $300 a month more simply because she chose to get married. Worker C sees you paying $400 to a peer and feels you are taking advantage of him just because he and his wife have other coverage. Worker B, though clearly innocent, may be resented by her co-workers for having a better deal.

To keep control of benefits costs, I elected to establish a fixed ben-

---

[1]At the time of this writing, there is no national health care program in the United States and no legislation requiring employers to provide a given level of coverage to their workers, although it is expected within the next year. Should such a program be enacted, it would certainly change the way Prototype Restaurants (and any employer, for that matter) will have to handle benefits. Please contact the author for his most current thinking in this area.

efit contribution per hour worked. This provides protection for the company as the cost of benefit plans increases. You may have already seen how easy it is to get squeezed by agreeing to pay a fixed percentage of the cost of a program.

A final provision in the interest of equity allows workers to apply the benefit contribution to any benefit program offered by the company. If any workers do not want any of the company's programs, they can choose to have their benefit payment made into a tax-sheltered savings (TSS) account, also known as a 401(k) plan.

The full policy on benefits contributions is included in Figure 7-1.

BENEFITS CONTRIBUTIONS (HR–408)

PROTOTYPE RESTAURANTS makes contributions for staff benefits based on the number of hours you work. This provides an equal treatment for all regular staff, regardless of the number of hours worked per week.

ELIGIBILITY
Only regular staff are eligible for benefits contributions.

AMOUNT OF CONTRIBUTION
The company makes benefits contributions for all regular staff on the following basis:

Hours 1–2,000	$0.45 per hour worked
Hours 2,001–8,000	$0.50 per hour worked
Hours 8,001–14,000	$0.55 per hour worked
Over 14,001 hours	$0.60 per hour worked

Upon acceptance as regular staff, your hours account will include all hours from your original date of hire. The company will make contributions only on hours worked *after* you receive regular staff status.

Figure 7-1   Benefits Contributions Policy
(from the Prototype Restaurants Staff Manual)

APPLICATION OF BENEFIT CONTRIBUTIONS

You may choose to have the contribution amount applied to your health plan, life insurance plan or paid to your TSS.

EMPLOYMENT STATUS

Benefit contributions depend on hours worked. Leave, paid or unpaid, is not hours worked. Therefore, the company will not make benefit contributions on your behalf during paid or unpaid leave. While you are on leave:

1. Health insurance, if you are enrolled, will continue. However, you must make 100% of the premium payments during the leave.

2. If you are a participant in the voluntary life insurance program, you must continue to make the premium payments.

3. If you are a participant in any other programs, it will be your responsibility to keep up all scheduled contributions.

Conditions covered in this section, items 1–3, do not apply beyond the approved leave of absence.

Figure 7-1 *(continued)*

TIME OFF

When I was working for a previous employer, all regular staff would automatically receive seven days sick leave at the beginning of the year and would accrue vacation based on the number of weeks worked. Upon leaving the company, a departing worker would be paid for any accrued vacation. Unused sick leave could be accumulated but would not be paid at the time of departure. Most of my crew did not believe they could ever have an extended illness, and since unused sick leave was not paid, building a big leave balance had no appeal. The predictable result was that everyone made it a point to be "sick" exactly seven days every year. Workers who planned to leave would wait until after the first of the year for the leave to be posted, have a sudden illness to use up the seven paid days, and then resign. In practice, the system rewarded people for being sick, not for staying healthy.

In designing a system for my own operations, the goal was to correct this flaw while assuring that all members of the staff would be treated equitably. There are three important elements of the solution:

1. **Make all leave the same.**   Time off is time off, whether for illness, vacation, or personal reasons. The only difference is when and how the worker gets approval to be gone. Eliminating the distinction between sick leave and vacation time simplifies the system, has no adverse impact on the company, and allows the staff to use their earned time off as they see fit.

2. **Accrue leave based only on hours worked.**   The relationship of time earned to hours worked assures that full-time and part-time workers receive equal treatment. It also avoids the problems that come with allocating a fixed amount of sick leave at the beginning of the year.

3. **Pay staff for any unused leave.**   This is the only fair way to handle leave. It encourages the staff not to take time off unless they really need it by allowing them to "cash in" unused leave at the hourly rate they are earning when they leave the company.

For an example of how these points might be handled in your manuals, see Figure 7-2.

PERSONAL LEAVE (HR–602)

We believe that time off is time off. Vacation, personal leave and sick time are all essentially the same. The company's personal leave formula provides time off benefits based on the number of hours you work. Whether used for vacation, personal time or illness, all earned leave is personal leave.

Figure 7-2   Leave Policy
(from the Prototype Restaurants Staff Manual)

Personal leave *accrues* (builds up) based on the following formula:

Hours 1–4,000	One hour off for every 30 hours worked.
Hours 4,001–8,000	One hour off for every 25 hours worked.
Hours 8,001–14,000	One hour off for every 20 hours worked.
Hours 14,001–20,000	One hour off for every 15 hours worked.
Over 20,001 hours	One hour off for every 10 hours worked.

The company posts accrued leave to your personal leave account at the end of the following Period. Accrued personal leave becomes *earned* only when posted. For example, personal leave accrued during Period 1 is posted (and therefore earned) at the end of Period 2. You cannot take personal leave (it is not yours) until it is earned.

You must request personal leave in writing at least three weeks (15 working days) in advance. The exception is for personal leave used for sickness. Coaches will approve or deny personal leave within five working days. Do not purchase non-refundable airline tickets without an approved leave request.

SICK LEAVE AND EXTENDED MEDICAL LEAVE (HR–603)

PROTOTYPE RESTAURANTS does not provide sick leave as such. We believe in incentives for people to stay healthy. However, you may use your earned personal leave for illness. We treat personal leave for illness (called sick leave) separately since the procedures for its use differ from personal leave. Sick leave is an approved period of absence from work, with or without pay, for medical reasons.

Figure 7-2 *(continued)*

You may use earned personal leave for illness, medical emergencies and non-job related injuries. You may also use earned personal leave for medical, psychological, dental or optical examinations or treatments. Paid sick leave cannot exceed the total number of earned personal leave hours.

If you are sick, you must call in your illness to the coach on duty before your regularly scheduled reporting time. Since you know you are going to be absent before your shift starts, a delay in calling in creates an unauthorized absence except in extreme cases. You *must* talk with the coach if the coach is in the building.

If you cannot talk to a coach, leave a message and phone number. When in doubt about whether you are well enough to work, come in and see how it goes. Your coach will send you home if it's not working.

When you are away from the job due to illness for three consecutive days, you must bring in a physician's statement before you can go back to work. We watch for pattern absences—repeatedly calling in sick on the same day, typically just before or after regularly scheduled days off. The second time this happens, expect a counseling session and a note in your file. We may require that you submit notes from your doctor for future absences that fit the pattern. Our purpose is not to penalize you for being sick but to address suspected misuse of the time off policies.

Extended absences for medical reasons, whether planned or unplanned, require a physician's statement. You must also get a physician's statement before you can return to work. Please advise your coach immediately when you know you will be off work for an extended period. In cases of medical emergencies, please advise your coach as soon as possible.

Figure 7-2 *(continued)*

Chapter Eight

Create a Sense of Motion

I would say training is probably the most important aspect of re-
duced turnover, because it minimizes mistakes and that minimizes a
lot of the reasons for turnover.
              —Stephen Hickey, Senior VP, TGI Friday's

At the age of 14, I was hired by a small restaurant on Cape Cod for
my first job—washing dishes (by hand!) during the summer tourist
season. The training for my frightening new responsibilities was
concise and pointed. It consisted of a single sentence: "Get back
there and do it!" This was followed by one sentence of counseling:
"And if you screw up, you're on the street."

Like most teenagers in the days before home dishwashing ma-
chines, I had *lots* of dishwashing experience, so that part of the job
was pretty easy. But I still remember my terror the first time I was
pointed in the general direction of the cleaning gear and told to
mop the floor. Talk about confusion! I had never even *seen* a string
mop before. We certainly didn't use one at home, so I had no idea
what it was or how to use it. My boss had me so terrified of making
a mistake that I didn't dare reveal my ignorance by asking him to
show me what to do.

Fortunately, Manny, one of the breakfast cooks, saw the terror in
my eyes and took me under his wing. He taught me how to mop the
floor and worked with me until I had mastered it. In addition to

being my mentor, he also became my inspector, making me re-do anything that didn't meet his standard, while making sure I understood why it was important to do it a certain way. Manny was tough, but he really cared how I did and believed in my ability to do a first-class job. Almost single-handedly, he helped me make a success of my first adventure in employment.

Manny was about the only first-class thing about that restaurant, and I often wonder whether I would have been "bitten by the restaurant bug" if it hadn't been for him. Thinking back about the experience, it is interesting to realize that I can still remember Manny, but the names of the boss and the restaurant have long since slipped from my memory.

A SENSE OF MOTION

The kind of people you want to build your organization on—the achievers and the keepers—need to feel like they are getting somewhere. This means that not only are they regularly increasing their income, but that they are making progress in their lives. In fact, personal and professional development can often be more satisfying than just monetary rewards, particularly in organizations where raises are handed out in an attempt to make up for past management abuses.

> If you can't pay the highest wage in town, you should at least offer the best vocational training program around.

This premise was one of the keys to the success of the foodservice program at the Olympic Training Center. We were not paying the highest wages in our market. We were a non-commercial operation with a strict salary administration system that did not give us the option of paying more money to workers who made larger contributions to our success. What we *could* offer prospective staff members, however, was an environment within which they could learn and advance their professional skills. We would teach them as much as they wanted to learn and give them as much responsibility as they were capable of handling, provided they were willing to meet our standards.

We built cross-training into the system so that everyone was learning each other's jobs. In effect, every member of the staff became a student as well as a teacher. Some did better than others. Some (usually the ones who wanted to get away with something) found the system was not to their liking and left. But no one could deny that the working environment was exciting and challenging.

I mentioned earlier that our turnover rate went from 300 percent to about 25 percent in six months. I believe our emphasis on training and staff development was a big factor in that success.

TRAINING AND TURNOVER

A recent study at Kansas State University examined the employees of a national fast food chain to investigate variables that might influence their intentions to remain in a job for longer periods of time. The variable having the greatest effect on an employee's length of employment related to training. The survey results suggest that as skill levels and job knowledge increased, employees' length of employment seemed to increase.

More than simply increasing professional skills, training raises people's level of certainty and personal security. In contrast, if you throw people into a situation for which they are totally untrained or unprepared, they may panic and freeze because of their insecurity.

THE COST OF TRAINING

Now I know that many operators feel that a training program is just too expensive, particularly when their staff turns over so quickly. A popular service trainer puts the dilemma into perspective when he poses a pair of rhetorical questions: "What if I train them and they leave? What if I *don't* train them and they *stay?*"

Many operators maintain that the most expensive training is no training at all. As one multi-unit operator put it, "When I don't train I only guarantee dissatisfied guests, high turnover and low productivity. I can't even begin to calculate the real price of this failure, but it has to be a thousand times greater than the cost of training."

Any foodservice professional knows that you cannot make quality products with substandard components. To continue the analogy, even the highest-quality ingredients will not satisfy your guests until they are modified and combined by following a good recipe. Left alone, high-quality ingredients will eventually just become high-quality compost!

It is the same with foodservice workers. Quality people are the primary ingredient in exemplary guest service. Left alone, they will spoil. Think of training as the recipe for getting the best from your staff. The better the recipe, the greater the resultant productivity and service. Most managers know that they should train more, but there are always reasons why they are not doing more of it. The common excuses are that there just isn't time or money. That rationalization is acceptable until you understand why there isn't enough time or money. Consider the possibility that there isn't enough time because the manager is too busy solving problems created by untrained workers. Perhaps there isn't enough money because sales are suffering from indifferent service delivered by an untrained staff. Get the picture?

Smart operators train their workers because they know their guests are worth the effort. Training is a logical extension of their guest-focused service mentality. Service-oriented operators also train to their own professional standards because they understand that it is dangerous to blindly assume that a worker's previous experience is relevant to the way they want their operations to run.

Following this premise, many restaurateurs prefer to build their service staffs from willing workers with a ready smile and no prior foodservice background. Inexperienced servers have no resistance to doing things exactly the way you want them done. Often "experienced workers" must first unlearn all the bad habits they picked up in their previous jobs before they can really meet your standards. This re-training process can be time-consuming and traumatic for everyone involved.

KNOW WHO SHOULD BE TRAINED

As a word of caution, consider the notion that not all people need training. Every once in awhile, you will run across a "natural"—a worker with sparkle, charisma, and a natural sense of what it takes to give your guests a memorable time under any circumstances. When you find a natural, don't try to tell them what to do. With these people, limit your training to procedures (such as operating the POS system) and activities where they have a specific interaction with other workers (such as placing orders at the bar). If you try to train a natural, you will either destroy their effectiveness or lose the worker.

Now before you are tempted to declare that all of your staff are natural talents as an excuse not to train them, consider reality. If you are fortunate, you may run across one or two naturals a year! So what can you do to help bring the rest of your crew up to the professional standards you have set for your operation? Since the majority of foodservice workers do not come by their skills naturally, it is your responsibility to train them. The question is how to do it.

GET SERIOUS ABOUT TRAINING

I am fortunate to know many excellent full-time trainers in the foodservice industry. They work primarily for multi-unit or large-volume operators and can concentrate almost exclusively on training—a luxury that most independent operators do not enjoy. For the operator without a training department, the prospect of creating an effective training program can seem intimidating. However, the following points will provide a clearer understanding of the fundamental steps in the process. Let's take a brief look at some of the elements of training that the non-trainer should understand.

1. Have a Plan

A successful training program is organized to impart proficiency in those areas that can be taught. Job skills, professional knowledge, company procedures, and work priorities are all valid topics for a training program. In setting up a training program, ask yourself the following questions. What does new (and present) staff have to know to be successful? How are they going to learn it? Who is going to help them learn it? How can you tell if the training was successful?

Once you have answered these questions, commit your plan to writing. Briefly outline the content, goals, materials, and audience for each session. Be realistic. Limit each classroom training period to one or two key points that can be handled in 20 to 45 minutes. Bear in mind that people assimilate new ideas best when the training comes in small doses. While it is ideal to have several hours of uninterrupted time to train, this is not realistic in most operations. It is better to design a program you know you can adhere to rather than to regularly cancel training sessions for lack of time. A sporadic program delivers a clear message about how important you feel training is to the success of your organization—and it may not be the message you want to send.

Your Dad probably told you to use the right tool for the right job. It is no different with training. All instruction methods are not equally effective. Video programs are a good way to impart ideas and approaches but are an ineffective way to teach physical skills. Role-playing or hands-on practice is the best method of teaching physical or interactive skills because people learn to do things by doing things. Printed material works well for learning company procedures. Group discussions and outside speakers will help workers develop perspective. Each has its place in an effective training program. Using a variety of training methods will help keep your trainees' interest and attention.

In designing your program, recognize that personal bearing, attitude, values, intelligence, and behavior patterns typically cannot be taught by training. For example, don't waste time trying to train people how to smile and be pleasant. If you want a friendly, outgoing staff, you have to select applicants who like people and who smile naturally.

As with all other decisions in the operation, develop your training program with the needs of your guests in mind. Be sure you understand your patrons' idea of exemplary service and that you are training to meet the needs of your guests. Don't automatically assume you know what they want. To illustrate, many operators reasonably assume that a friendly, outgoing staff is an important factor in guest gratification—and in most operations it is. However, a Taco Bell study determined that their customers primarily wanted food served correctly, hot, and fast. The smiles and extra touches that are so important in full-service restaurants were not what Taco Bell patrons wanted. Similarly, KFC found that in some inner-city locations, "bubbly" counter staff were not appreciated. The client base thought the behavior was phony and some even thought the staff member was "coming on" to them.

On-the-job (OJT) training is perhaps the most common industry learning format. "Follow Carol and she'll show you what to do" is a valid training method, provided that Carol knows how you want things done and that she, in fact, does them that way. Too often, these "shadow shifts" are just a way for one worker to teach their bad habits to another. Even OJT has to have a plan. Make a checklist for both the trainer and the trainee so that both will be clear about exactly what is being taught, what standards of behavior are expected, and how they will be measured.

One industry consultant offered a novel twist on the idea of OJT for service staff. He suggests having the new server wait on the staff and serve them the employee meal. The "guests" in this scenario could either be the veteran servers or the top staff members. The apprentice follows the restaurant's guest service sequence and the staff members offer their comments and critique after the meal. The program can last as long as management likes. There is an obvious benefit to new servers, who can gain honest feedback and polish their technique before facing the public. The restaurant's guests benefit because management no longer asks diners to help train rookie servers. Those who benefit most, however, are often the veterans who have a chance to experience the restaurant's service first-hand. Their involvement in the training process helps them better understand the guest's perspective and makes them more sensitive to the needs of their patrons.

2. Impart Perspective

Our model of education is based primarily on the transfer of information and certainly it is better to know specific information than not to know it. Still, training that stops with knowledge can be ineffective. The real power comes from understanding. Understanding is knowing how to use knowledge—what we might call perspective.

Truly effective training will give the trainees perspective on their job and the operation. Toward this end, it is helpful that people not only understand how to do their job, but how their job relates to the overall goal of the operation—making every guest happy. It also helps staff members gain perspective when they understand the jobs of others in the company, how their job affects the performance of their co-workers, and how the overall operation works. Responsive "front counter" service cannot happen unless the people at the front counter know how everything works in the back of the house. When they are conversant with all areas of the operation, they will then know exactly who to talk to or what to do if there is a problem or service snag.

One very effective way to make sure that your staff understands all aspects of the operation is to require all new hires to work in other departments of the restaurant before settling into their final jobs. If you only worry about cross-training within each department, you may be missing an opportunity. Once you start to give everyone a taste of reality in the kitchen, dining room, patio and bar, you will find that their attitudes really improve. Expect a staff that is better informed, has more pride in the restaurant, and can answer most guest questions from personal experience. This translates into a higher level of service for your diners and that is what this business is all about.

Workers need to understand the reasons behind your service procedures, particularly when handling complaints. Statistics indicate that as many as 14 percent of dissatisfied guests do not return because their complaints were not handled properly. A staff member who understands the reasoning behind your procedures and policies and the importance of happy guests to your success is better equipped to resolve problems in a way that meets the needs of both the guest and the house.

As a final point, trainees should have some input into their training. This premise also suggests that a lecture will be more effective when followed by a discussion. Discussion allows everyone in the class to participate and helps workers reach their own understanding of the material. It helps if you approach training sessions as a coach would. Coaches understand that the talent already resides in their players. The job of the coach is just to bring out and direct these abilities in the interest of providing exemplary guest service.

3. Set a Personal Example

Personal example speaks most clearly. Your staff will treat guests the same way they are treated and they will do what they see you doing. If training for service does not reflect the reality of the restaurant, you might as well throw it out the window. Don't teach your staff ways of working with customers if those methods are not supported by the management team. Service training starts at the top of the organization, not from the bottom up. In order for people to serve the customer, they need to feel supported and "serviced" by their management team. This applies all the way up the organizational ladder.

Personal example is the best teacher. To get their crew excited about learning, top managers must show that they are seriously (and eagerly) pursuing their own professional advancement. To keep their staff open to new ideas, managers should realize that they do not know everything and that it is permissible (and positive) to learn from their workers. I also recommend that managers be involved in their local and national trade associations, attend industry shows, and participate in educational programs. How else are they going to find the new ideas that will keep them growing? Trainers, too, may have to look outside the organization for professional development. Professional curiosity is contagious and is spread by personal example.

What you learn is often less important than the fact that you are learning. The implication is that the best way to change your staff's behavior is to change your own! It is the easiest thing you can do to foster interest in training. "I couldn't understand why everybody in the organization seemed to resist learning anything new," confessed a recent participant in one of my seminars. "Then it occurred to me that it had been several years since I had done anything to improve my own understanding of the business. As soon as I started attending seminars offered by the state restaurant association, my restaurant's staff turned their attitudes around totally. I never had to say a word. Learning is now an integral part of our operating style." Is it worth it? I talked with this person recently and he reported that his turnover was down and his sales for the first quarter of the year were up 30 percent!

4. Offer a Career Path, Not Just a Job

Anyone can offer a job but few foodservice employers take enough interest in their staff to actually create a career path for them. By career path I mean showing new workers, whether at the entry level or more advanced, where the starting job can lead and how you will help them get there.

The model I always go back to is Scouting. When I joined the Cub Scouts, I got a book that told me what the various ranks were and what I had to do to achieve each of them. Along the way there were badges and ceremonies to give me encouragement as I advanced. I was also surrounded by mentors and role models whose job it was to help me achieve all the success I wanted. I had a great time, all the while knowing that I would soon be too old for Cub Scouts and there was a bigger game waiting for me.

When I was old enough to become a Boy Scout, I started at the bottom of the ladder again, but I already knew how to play the game. Again the steps in the advancement path were clear and the support organization was in place. I could advance just as quickly as I could demonstrate the required proficiencies and pass the appropriate tests.

As I advanced, my progress was recognized in front of my peers with award ceremonies and each success made me more eager for the next one. Everyone in the troop had the same opportunities to win and whether or not someone took advantage of them was strictly up to them. The older boys helped the younger boys and the adults helped everyone. It was very understandable and great fun.

This is not to suggest that we should develop foodservice merit badges or sing songs around the campfire (although it might be something to think about!). Still, there are some basic truths in the Scouting model that we can use to do a better job of creating a career path for our staff. Here are some points to include when setting up advancement ladders for your crew:

Set clear objectives. Create a map of your organization—identify where each job fits into the next and to what stage you can progress from every position in the company. The objectives should also spell out what skills and knowledge are required at each step of the process and how each will be measured. Review this material with new workers either as part of their orientation or within a few weeks of their starting work. Find out what they want to accomplish in their lives (or at least in terms of what they know at the moment) and show them how the organization can help them meet their personal goals. This is a critical and essential first step.

Develop the training to meet the objectives. Once people know where they can go, we must provide the vehicle to help them get there if they want to make the trip. How will we impart the skills and knowledge? Is it all learned on the job or do we expect them to pick up part of it on their own? If so, how?

Provide rewards and recognition. If the primary thing workers want from their jobs is recognition for the work that they do, we can give it to them in the training program. As they reach each new skill level, as they receive promotions, as they demonstrate exceptional advancement, we can recognize these important growth steps with rewards and public recognition. Some of the rewards may be monetary ones—many should be—but it is equally important just to let people know that you noticed what they did and that they did it well.

Some companies denote skill levels in the kitchen by the color of the scarf that the individual wears. Perhaps the color of their nametag changes as front-of-the-house workers advance. Mentors might be denoted by a special pin. Particular proficiencies might also be denoted by a special pin, such as one given to those who had passed a CPR course or been declared Certified Servers by virtue of demonstrating particular skill and knowledge. Whatever form it takes, reward and recognition is what creates the sense of motion.

Build in peer support. Assign each new worker a mentor or a buddy, a person who is a more experienced member of your staff and whose responsibility it is to help the newcomer adjust to the company and support their professional development. When the chemistry is right, the mentor becomes a coach, a teacher, a confidante, a guide, and a sounding board. The mentor's job is not to make the new person successful, because everyone is ultimately responsible for their own success. A mentor makes the trip less intimidating.

Consider the full spectrum of training. Training is anything that helps a person learn. In addition to in-house programs, training can also include outside seminars sponsored by the state restaurant association or suppliers and attendance at industry trade shows. Training can even include reimbursed visits to competitors' operations.

Provide organizational support. How did we ever get the idea that our organizations could win if our people didn't? The only way we can improve is to have our staff improve, even if this means that they will leave us for positions of higher authority elsewhere. Face it: they will leave eventually no matter what we do. Even so, it is far better to have them motivated and excited while they still are with us.

5. Monitor Your Results

Training without monitoring and followup is almost useless. Just as you can only define good service from the guest's point of view, you can only measure effective training by the performance of the trainee. In other words, if the student has not learned, the teacher has not taught.

Your training program should be designed to produce *measurable* results. You must, in fact, measure them because what you measure is what you will get. You can give tests to measure knowledge, you can track sales figures, tally server errors, monitor response times, and generally provide feedback on performance. You do not have to beat anyone over the head with statistics. Usually, simply posting the measurements without comment is the most effective way to deliver the message. Good foodservice workers are naturally competitive and they will work to exceed a goal. All they have to know is where they are now and what level of performance they are trying to reach.

As you take measurements, be sure to recognize and encourage staff members who are applying what they learned in the training. If they are making mistakes, remind them of everything that is being done properly and then coach them on the areas that can be done better. Like it or not, your operating style is also part of your training program. If it is not okay to make mistakes, people won't even try something new. Remember that coaches focus on strengths while cops look for problems. Do you approach training like a coach—or like a cop?

USE EFFECTIVE TRAINERS

In most independent operations and in many multi-unit companies, the foodservice managers are also the principal trainers. So how good a trainer *are* you? To get an idea of your training savvy, complete the quiz at the end of the chapter and use the results as a guide on how you can get even better.

To grade the effectiveness of your training program, consider the following questions:

- Does it involve every member of the staff and management?
- Is it participatory?

- Do you use a variety of training methods to avoid boredom?
- Do the trainees have a say in what sort of training they receive?
- Is it consistently administered rather than hit-or-miss?
- Have you established clear goals for each part of the training?
- Do you regularly measure and post the results of training?
- Is the desired behavior consistently reinforced and rewarded?

For some specific training outlines, you might want to look at *The Restaurant Training Program*, by Karen Eich Drummond (see "Resources for Retention"). If these comments start you rethinking the issue of training, I have accomplished my purpose. It helps to recognize training as an investment in happy guests, higher retention, and improved profits. When times get tough, savvy organizations of all sizes intensify their training activities rather than scaling them back in an attempt to save money. They realize that downsizing the training function is counterproductive and a sign of false economy. Training, like service, is a state of mind.

As a final thought, consider a slogan from the National Education Association:

> If you think training is expensive, try ignorance!

WHAT'S IN IT FOR ME?

It is easy to see how the organization will benefit from increasing the skill level and effectiveness of its staff, but the motivating factor for your crew is what will be in it for them. Expanding one's professional competence has value, but if newfound capabilities are not recognized with bonuses, raises, or promotions within a reasonable period of time, your good workers may feel they have reached a dead end in your organization and start looking for opportunities elsewhere.

To keep workers interested over the long term, there has to be a clear answer to the question of "What's in it for me?" Specific programs will depend on the structure of your organization. In an ideal world, pay would be based on demonstrated competencies. While this may not be realistic in most operations, perhaps you might offer a bonus for demonstrated proficiency in a new area of training.

A sure indication that there is light at the end of the tunnel is when vacancies are (or can be) filled by promotion of a current member of the staff. If internal promotion is not possible, management must ask three questions: "Why not?," "Who is the most likely candidate when the opening comes up again?" and "What will it take for them to be ready the next time?" When you have the answers to these questions, you have the basis for an intense professional development program.

The key to keeping people involved is showing them that you are committed to their success. There may not be opportunities for advancement within the organization every time you have a person who is ready to advance. In these cases, demonstrating your commitment to your people may mean helping place them with a competitor. At first glance, this idea may sound incredible. However, consider that a person caught in a dead end will gradually become resentful, less productive, and bring down the climate of the entire company before (inevitably) leaving. We have already discussed the power of climate. In contrast, the enthusiasm and trust you will inspire by demonstrating such a commitment to your staff as individuals will build loyalty and support from your crew and keep the work environment positive. In the long run, you have more to gain than you have to lose. To keep the "win-win" relationship going when you provide a star worker to another operator who needs one, you may be able to ask for another good worker in exchange. It's worth a try.

TEST YOURSELF AS A TRAINER

To determine your qualities as a trainer, mark the following questions "True" or "False" based on your personal understanding of training and how it works.

T   F

☐   ☐   1. The restaurant has an obligation to provide staff members with the skills necessary to do their jobs.

☐   ☐   2. Staff turnover is often related to training, or the lack of it.

☐   ☐   3. Learning on-the-job is not the only way to provide necessary learning for new employees.

☐   ☐   4. Training low-skilled workers may be just as important as training highly skilled people.

☐   ☐   5. Prior to training, explain company rules and regulations to the new worker.

☐   ☐   6. Prior to training, answer the unspoken question in every trainee's mind: "What's in it for me?"

☐   ☐   7. Popular workers usually make good trainers.

☐   ☐   8. Before actual training begins, explain the position as it relates to the total operation of the restaurant.

☐   ☐   9. A person who performs well on the job is qualified to teach others the skills needed for the job.

☐   ☐   10. The ability to train can be developed to a large extent.

☐   ☐   11. A trainer should spend at least as much time getting things ready for training as in actual instruction.

☐   ☐   12. The trainer should know the desired results to be achieved before beginning to teach and should list the key points around which the instruction will be built.

Figure 8-1

☐ ☐ 13. The trainer should learn what the student already knows about the subject before starting to train.

☐ ☐ 14. The trainer should have an organized plan and know the amount of learning that is expected day-by-day.

☐ ☐ 15. In setting instructional goals, give trainees more work than they can accomplish to demonstrate that you have high standards.

☐ ☐ 16. When a trainee performs correctly, reward the person with praise, something like "That's good," or "You're doing fine."

☐ ☐ 17. A trainer must never admit past or present errors or not knowing an answer to a question.

☐ ☐ 18. The best way to handle a cocky trainee is to put them down in front of others.

☐ ☐ 19. In training new workers, concentrate upon speed rather than form.

☐ ☐ 20. Surprise quizzes and examinations are good ways to ensure high-level performance.

☐ ☐ 21. Expect that there will be periods during the training when no observable progress is made.

☐ ☐ 22. Expect some people to learn two or three times as fast as others.

☐ ☐ 23. Both tell and show the trainee how to perform the skill you are training.

☐ ☐ 24. When a trainee performs incorrectly, say, "No, not that way."

☐ ☐ 25. After a task has been learned, ask trainees for suggestions as to how to improve the task.

Source: Donald E. Lundberg, *The Restaurant from Concept to Operation*, pp. 153–155, © 1985 by John Wiley & Sons, Inc., adapted with permission.

Figure 8-1 *(continued)*

TEST ANSWERS

1. T   One of the best summaries of the importance of training comes from Hap Gray, owner of the Watermark Restaurant in Cleveland. He says, "My training program is what makes this *my* restaurant. If I did not train my staff, I would only be a caretaker for the bank."

2. T   Untrained people never understand what they are expected to do or how to do it. This leads to mistakes and negative feedback from management, both major factors in turnover.

3. T   While learning on the job is certainly part of most workers' skill development, it is not the only form of training.

4. T   The only way that low-skilled workers even get to *be* highly skilled is through training!

5. T   To create learner interest explain the benefits that accrue to the person. Set the record straight by explaining the rules and regulations of the company. All of the benefits and the requirements should be explained and out of the way before skill training is started.

6. T   People do what they do for their own reasons. Helping them see how training will benefit them personally gives them a vested interested in its success.

7. F   Popularity does not necessarily correlate highly with being a good trainer.

8. T   It is important to see the particular job as a part of the whole.

9. F   The ability to teach is a skill distinctly separate from professional performance.

10. F   Unfortunately, not everyone has the personality to be effective trainers. While it is certainly possible for trainers to improve their effectiveness, qualities like desire, caring, patience and empathy—important qualities of an effective trainer—are not typically talents that can be trained.

Figure 8-1 *(continued)*

11. T It is important for the instructor to be properly prepared. Inadequate preparation is unprofessional and makes the trainees less secure about what they are learning.

12. T Knowing this information gives trainees a context for what will follow and aids in their learning.

13. T To maintain interest, the level of the training should be compatible with the knowledge and skills of the trainee. Without this knowledge, it is easy to talk over the head of those with no knowledge or bore more advanced students. In either case, very little effective transfer of information occurs.

14. T This helps keep the training on track and increases the trainees' confidence in the process.

15. F Training is an occasion when success at every step is important. Standards should be set which are achievable and avoid the experience of failure.

16. T Positive reinforcement validates the trainee and encourages continued learning.

17. F No one expects a perfect trainer (except perhaps an *imperfect* trainer!).

18. F Even though a trainee is out of line, it does no good to embarrass the person. Rather, talk to the person privately.

19. F Form comes first, speed comes later.

20. F Surprises are not considered good in training.

21. T There are times when consolidation of skills takes place and no observable progress is made.

22. T There is a vast range of individual differences found in the general population.

23. T Different people learn in different ways. Covering all the bases helps assure that your training will "stick."

24. F This is a negative way of teaching. Far better to emphasize the positive.

25. T Every task can be improved by new techniques, new methods, new equipment, new skills. Or, it may be completely eliminated as unnecessary.

Figure 8-1 *(continued)*

Chapter Nine

Show Your Appreciation

What is it most of us want from work? We would like to find the most effective, most productive, most rewarding way of working together. We would like a work process and relationships that meet our personal needs for belonging, for contributing, for meaningful work, for the opportunity to make a commitment, for the opportunity to grow and be at least reasonably in control of our own destinies. Finally, we'd like someone to say "Thank you!"

    —Max De Pree, CEO, Herman Miller, Inc.

Do you get all the appreciation you deserve for everything you do for people? Few of us do. Perhaps, as a consequence, we seldom think to give our staff all the recognition they deserve, either. Since all staff surveys tell us that the primary thing that people want from their jobs is appreciation for the work that they do, why don't we do it more often?

If you are serious about improving your retention, you have to do a better job of regularly showing your staff how much you value their contributions. This means building appreciation into your operating system. If you don't, you will only fall back into the hit-or-miss mode you are probably using now. "Catching people doing something right" is a powerful way to reinforce the behavior you want while making your staff feel more secure on the job.

REWARD THE BEHAVIOR YOU WANT

In his classic book, *The Greatest Management Principle in the World*, (see "Resources for Retention"), Dr. Michael LeBoeuf points out that people behave the way the reward system teaches them to behave. If you want to know why you are getting a particular behavior, take a look at what is being rewarded.

A wonderful example of the power of this technique is teaching pigeons to bowl! You may not have heard of it, but there are pigeons who will walk up to a small ball, knock it straight down an alley, and hit some little bowling pins. How, you ask eagerly, can I possibly teach a pigeon to do that? The process is intriguing.

You start with a hungry pigeon, a ball, the alley, and the pins. The pigeon first gets a reward when it *looks* at the ball. Then it is rewarded when it takes a step in the direction of the ball. You know how pigeons bob up and down a bit when they walk? Well, the next reward comes as the bird is bobbing downward while stepping toward the ball. Then it is rewarded when it touches the ball, then when it moves the ball, and then when it moves the ball roughly in the direction of the pins. The "reward angle" gradually gets smaller until the pigeon is knocking the ball straight down the alley.

Do you know how long it takes to teach a pigeon to do that? Trainers say it can usually be done in about fifteen minutes! Think about the process. The only time the bird gets a reward is when it makes progress in the direction you want it to go. All other behavior is ignored. When do you reward your staff with *your* attention?

It is important to recognize and reward any progress your staff makes in the direction you want them to go. To the extent possible, ignore all other actions. Remember that what gets rewarded is what gets done. Are you the typical manager who usually only comments on staff errors or behavior that moves *away* from the desired results? If so, accept the consequence that there may be members of your staff who are making mistakes because that is the only way they get acknowledged!

Following this principle, one way to help reduce your turnover is to reward managers for improving their staff retention statistics as we discussed in Chapter 2, rather than chewing them out for the number of people who leave. Here are a few other behaviors (or movement toward these behaviors) you might want to acknowledge:

- reporting to work on time
- neat, clean appearance
- exceptional effort
- taking the initiative to resolve a problem
- exceptional personal service to guests
- cost-saving suggestions
- referrals to fill a staff vacancy
- meticulous sanitation practices

For a greater insight into the power of rewards, you might also want to read *Don't Shoot the Dog* (see "Resources for Retention") by Karen Pryor, a former trainer at Hawaii's Sea Life Park. (The book title, by the way, comes from one method you can use to keep a dog from barking! Shooting the dog will certainly stop the barking, but there are other ways to do it.)

CUSTOMIZE THE REWARDS USED

A reward is not a reward unless it means something to the recipient. Different groups may have different hot buttons and a good coach will know what gets people excited. Not all rewards have to be monetary. For some of your staff, a Saturday night off might be more valuable than a cash bonus. Often, just a sincere "thank you" can work wonders.

When it comes to monetary rewards, a bonus is usually better than a raise. An extra five dollars to a cook at the end of a particularly busy night seems like a lot more money (and costs far less) than a ten-cent-an-hour raise. It also ties the reward directly to the behavior while keeping the base wage rates in line. Everybody knows how much money everybody else makes anyway and a raise for one will bring pressure for a similar increase from others.

TIE REWARDS TO PERFORMANCE

It is essential that rewards be based on demonstrated performance. Without a performance base, rewards can actually be a de-motivator. An example that comes to mind is a regional chain I know of that has a bonus program for their unit managers. In order to qualify for a bonus, the manager is supposed to achieve certain operating results. In practice, the company is reluctant to risk irritating a manager. The result is that every manager gets a bonus regardless of the results achieved. The bonus program has degenerated into a welfare system in which there is no added incentive for exceptional performance, the bonus is meaningless as a motivator, and the entire bonus system has become a joke. In fact, the high-performing managers actually resent the fact that the company provides equal rewards to the less-effective managers.

Chapter Ten

Keep Everyone Informed

Everybody must be judged on his performance, not on his looks or his manners or his personality or who he knows or is related to.
—Robert Townsend

Everybody hates your performance appraisal system.

Don't take it personally—that's just the way it usually is in most companies. Your managers hate it because it causes them to be judgmental and either to be painfully honest or to be wishy-washy in the interests of keeping peace in the family. Your staff hates it because they rarely feel they are getting the honesty or support they want from management. They know they are doing the best they can and they don't like finding out that their efforts are either misunderstood or unappreciated. They may also feel that their performance appraisal (and those of their co-workers) more accurately reflect the degree to which they have managed to stay on the good side of the boss, not the level of their professional performance.

Many independent operators try to side-step the issue by not engaging in performance appraisal at all. In practice, this is even more destructive to staff morale. The practice of "I'll let you know if you are screwing up," leaves workers in the dark as to what sort of job they are doing and continually looking over their shoulder for the attack they feel sure is coming. You can see how both reactions can make a person more insecure, lowering their state of mind which, in turn, lowers their productivity and increases their general dissatisfaction with both the company and their jobs.

Understand that the basic problem may be structural. Performance appraisals have a much poorer chance of success in the cop school of management. Since cops look for problems to fix, the appraisal process can easily become heavily weighted in favor of identifying shortcomings, setting deadlines, and instilling fear.

You can't play to win if you don't know the score and performance appraisals are an essential part of any formal feedback system. So how can we engage in a meaningful discussion with our workers? My suggestion to you is twofold: first, you will have better luck and create a more positive working environment if you change the way you define the positions in the organization. Having done that, you can then shift the way in which you conduct staff evaluations. But you can't do the second effectively without having done the first.

POSITION DESCRIPTIONS

At first glance, position descriptions may not seem like a part of a program to reduce turnover, but they are like a road map of your organization. Properly constructed, they help workers to better understand the game you are asking them to play. They also provide a context within which your staff can better understand how their jobs relate to the success of the operation. This makes their jobs meaningful and, in my experience, people with meaningful jobs are more likely to keep them.

The problem with most job descriptions is that they are little more than lists of activities and they don't really contribute to understanding or personal involvement. Several times in the past, I have worked in operations with activity-based descriptions and occasionally I had to conduct a performance appraisal for workers who were not meeting my standards. Invariably, they defended their performance by showing how they had, in fact, performed every task on their job description. This is akin to claiming to be the world's greatest lover by virtue of having memorized the manual. It is also about as effective!

Marvin's Law of Creative Laziness says that you never do any more work than necessary to accomplish what you want. Following this premise, my suggestion is that you describe positions in terms of *results* instead of *activities*. Defining results allows people to interpret their jobs in a way that works for them. If you call someone a server, they may think they have done the job if they simply serve! Describe the position in terms of the results to be achieved, however, and the whole game changes.

The immediate advantage is that workers become more involved in their jobs, which leads to increased productivity, enhanced guest service, improved morale, higher retention, and more constructive performance appraisals. Focusing on results also helps your staff become more involved with your company, which is another factor that will cause them to stay longer.

When developing results-based job descriptions, the basic questions to ask are these: *"If you were world class at what you do, how would we know it? What would you be doing? What would you be seeing? What would people be saying? What could we measure that would help us know that we are on track?"*

With these questions in mind, start to look at the job in terms of what you want to accomplish and don't concern yourself with how it has to happen. Any behavior you want to eliminate (and any behavior you want to encourage) can be flagged by identifying the results you want to achieve. For example, I am a stickler for sanitation and I wanted to see excellent health department inspections. Therefore, one of the results I used to evaluate a person's performance was whether health department scores were above 90, with no major violations in that person's department. Knowing that they would be evaluated on this result, people asked two questions: *"What does it take to get a 90 on the health inspection?"* and *"What is a major health department violation?"* Imagine how much easier it is to conduct sanitation classes when people are asking those two questions!

High turnover is more likely when the job is perceived as undesirable. The path to more desirable jobs in our industry may be to look at them in a different way. Results-based job descriptions can be a big help in shifting people's perception of their work. Figure 10-1 will give you an idea of what a results-based job description might look like. A more detailed discussion of this concept, along with sample write-ups for principal foodservice positions, is part of *The Foolproof Foodservice Selection System.*

PERFORMANCE APPRAISAL

In most systems, the manager typically takes on the role of judge in performance appraisal. A more productive role is that of facilitator,

---

Position: Service Manager
Mentor: Assistant Head Coach
Trains: Assistant Service Managers, Floor Managers

POSITION SUMMARY:

Delights restaurant patrons with responsive food and beverage service.

ESSENTIAL PROFESSIONAL FUNCTIONS:

- Sells and serves food and beverages to guests in the dining room and bar.
- Presents menus, answers questions, makes suggestions regarding food and beverages.
- Writes orders on guest checks.
- Relays orders to the service bar and kitchen.
- Serves courses from service bar and kitchen.
- Observes guests, anticipates needs and responds to additional requests.
- Accurately totals guest checks, accepts payment and makes change.
- Clears and resets tables.

Figure 10-1   Position Description

- Cleans the service areas as necessary.
- Inspects restrooms every 30 minutes and cleans as necessary.
- Conducts daily inspections of service areas.
- Creates effective training program for assistants.
- Recognizes and reports all necessary maintenance promptly.
- Fills in where needed to ensure efficient operations.
- Suggests improvements to the operating format.

RESULTS UPON WHICH PERFORMANCE IS EVALUATED:

- Guests are acknowledged within one minute of being seated.
- Food orders are delivered within one minute of completion.
- Average check meets or exceeds posted goals.
- Hot food is consistently served hot and cold food is consistently served cold.
- Guests have a spontaneous positive reaction when plate is presented.
- Health department scores exceed 90 with no major violations in the service department.
- Assistants are steadily improving their skills as measured by quarterly tests.
- Service staff vacancies are filled by internal promotions.
- Regularly attends training seminars.
- Stories of legendary guest service abound.
- Contributions are recognized by co-workers on peer appraisals.
- Guests comment favorably on the tastiness and presentation of meals.
- Service areas are always neat and clean.

Figure 10-1 *(continued)*

- Guests have a great time every time as measured by repeat patronage of 80–85%.
- Resolves guest problems (in favor of the guest) immediately.
- Knowledgeable on menu items, drinks and wines.
- Guests regularly ask for this staff member to serve them.
- Guests make unsolicited comments on the cleanliness of the restrooms.

QUALIFICATION STANDARDS:

- Able to operate a cash register or electronic POS system.
- Walks and stands during the entire shift.
- Reading and writing skills required.
- Reaches, bends, stoops, and wipes.
- Carries service tray weighing up to 30 pounds from kitchen to dining room about 24 times per shift.
- Interacts verbally with patrons.
- Hazards may include, but are not limited to, cuts, burns, slipping and tripping.

Figure 10-1 *(continued)*

reporter, or coach. Because we have identified the results we are trying to achieve, it becomes possible to coach. Coaches look for strengths to build on, so most of the discussions between the coaches and the crew focus on what is being done right and identifying the next area for the staff member to focus on improving.

This allows us to create more of a feedback system than a performance appraisal system. Feedback is important, but the basis should be some form of data collection, rather than just the subjective opinions of the management. Your ability to provide effective feedback requires that you have clear standards to measure against. Feedback based on established standards is less threatening to the staff, more positive for the coaches, and helps contribute to a productive working environment.

THE COACHING REPORT

Figure 10-2 shows a sample performance evaluation that utilizes the structure of the results-based position descriptions to make performance review as positive (and painless) as possible. Notice that it is called a Coaching Report. The way to use it should be self-explanatory, but here are a few hints. On the first page, list the key activities of the position (from the position description), the results desired, and the results observed. Remember that your role is that of facilitator, reporter, and coach. The results desired should be developed with the staff member either during the confirmation period or at their last performance appraisal session. Use the comments column to make notes of the points you want to discuss with the worker to assist in their professional development. On the second page of the Coaching Report, do the same with the key points from the "Results Upon Which Performance is Evaluated" section of the position description.

A world-class performance appraisal system must be multi-faceted. Certainly the management will rate each person's performance, but staff members should also rate their own performance as part of the process. To broaden the perspective, we can use comment cards and letters to get an idea of how our guests rate our workers' performances. Your staff can fool you, but they cannot fool their co-workers, so a meaningful feedback system should also allow workers to rate each other.[1] Figure 10-3 is a sample format for peer appraisal that I have used with success. When it is appraisal time, ask the person's co-workers to complete this form anonymously (and return them to a drop box), summarize the comments, and include them on page 3 of the Coaching Report.

To be fair, the system must also allow workers to comment on the

---

[1]You can see how a profit-sharing program would make this peer appraisal even more important for everyone. See Chapter 12 for more discussion on profit-sharing.

Prototype Restaurants
COACHING REPORT

Page 1

NAME: Susan, Service Manager	PERIOD COVERED: August 15 - February 14	REPORT PREPARED BY: Coach Pete

ACTIVITIES	RESULTS DESIRED	RESULTS OBSERVED	COMMENTS
Sells and serves food and beverage	smooth, seamless service	generally competent service	service can be uneven when rushed, relax and stay focused
Presents menus	menus open, right-side up	menus open, right-side up	eye contact and a smile when presenting menus - excellent!
Answers guest questions	never hear "I don't know"	some confusion on new items	study new items, work with mentor to fill in voids
Makes suggestions	personal recommendations	some descriptions memorized	doing much better, be sure to taste and talk from experience
Writes orders on guest checks	neat, legible, proper codes	neat, legible, proper codes	checks are perfect, makes it easier for the kitchen - super!
Relays orders to service bar and kitchen	orders get there w/in 60 seconds	OK during week, 2 min Fri/Sat	ask for help when getting behind
Serves courses from service bar and kitchen	service pace matches guest needs	generally appropriate pace	the key to reading the table is to drop distractions
Anticipates needs, responds to requests	guests never have to ask	improving	the key to reading the table is to drop distractions
Accurately totals guest checks	math is 100% accurate	all audited checks were perfect	exceptional math skills
Accepts payments, makes change	100% accuracy	accuracy good, style is still rough	face bills, count cash back to guest
Clears and resets tables	tables are reset within 3 minutes	average reset time: 4.25 minutes	note table status, time should improve as other skills are mastered
Cleans the service areas	always neat and clean	exceptionally clean service areas	does a great job of cleaning service areas
Inspects restrooms and cleans as necessary	positive guest comments	adequate job of cleaning	with a little extra effort, could make them sparkle
Conducts daily inspections of service area	always stocked and complete	some unnecessary shortages noted	it is time to work on anticipating supply needs
Creates effective training for assistants	assistants are advancing	not applicable	ready to take on training responsibilities
Recognizes/reports necessary maintenance	no unreported problems		no specific comments
Fills in where needed	supervisor never has to ask	misses opportunities to help	remember that we are all in this together
Suggests operational improvements	actively involved in the company	holds self out	needs to recognize the importance and value of her input

Figure 10-2

COACHING REPORT

Page 2

EVALUATION FACTORS	RESULTS DESIRED	RESULTS OBSERVED	COMMENTS
Newly-seated guests promptly acknowledged	within one minute of seating	average 75 seconds	ask for help when getting behind
Food orders delivered quickly	within one minute of completion	average 90 seconds	ask for help when getting behind
Average check meets or exceeds posted goals	$7.50 lunch, $13.50 dinner	$7.80 lunch, $13.45 dinner	good work/remember to build loyalty, not the check average
Hot food is consistently served hot	food temperature is over 150°	late delivery makes for cool food	need to get food to the table more quickly
Cold food is consistently served cold	food temperature is under 38°	generally OK	faster service would keep chill on the food
Guests are delighted with plate presentation	spontaneous positive reaction	spontaneous positive reaction	plate presentation skills are good
Health inspection scores are excellent	over 90 with no major violations	last inspection score 86	keep working on general sanitation awareness
Helps assistants to develop professionally	test scores are improving	not applicable	she is ready to take on training responsibility
Service staff ready for promotion	vacancies filled internally	not applicable	she is ready to take on training responsibility
Staff continues their professional education	attends training seminars	missed one seminar	understands the need for continuous improvement
Guests appreciate and notice the extra effort	guests comments are favorable	comments are generally favorable	guests appear to be satisfied, now we can work on guest delight!
Service areas are well-maintained	always neat and clean	exceptionally clean service areas	does a great job of cleaning service areas
Guests have a great time every time	repeat patronage is 80-85%	repeat patronage estimate: 60%	work on improving connection with guests and inviting them back
Guest problems are resolved quickly	immediately/in favor of the guest	generally handles problems well	very conscientious to resolve difficulties quickly
Knowledgeable on menu items, drinks, wines	never hear "I don't know"	some confusion on new items	study new items, work with mentor to fill in voids
Service is personal and memorable	guests ask for this server	two requests in this eval period	work on improving connection with guests and inviting them back
Guests are impressed w/restroom cleanliness	candid comments on cleanliness	doing acceptable cleaning job	delighting guests calls for doing more than expected

Figure 10-2 (*continued*)

Page 3

COACHING REPORT

Peer Appraisal

EVALUATION FACTORS	NEVER	SOMETIMES	USUALLY	ALWAYS	GENERAL PEER COMMENTS
Contributes to a positive atmosphere		7	12	14	fun to work with, can be moody, great smile
Uses time appropriately		14	15	4	ignores some guests and talks to others, long restroom breaks
Does their job right	1	8	11	13	very sharp, gets all the details
Is a good team player	1	11	12	9	makes me look good, looks out for herself first
Cares about their work		5	13	15	takes pride in what she does

General Comments and Suggestions from the Coaches

Figure 10-2 (*continued*)

Page 4

COACHING REPORT

Goals for Next Appraisal Period

Staff Member's Comments

My coach and I have discussed my performance including all the comments and suggestions above. I understand the reasoning behind all comments included in this report.

STAFF MEMBER: *Susan, Service Manager (signature)*   DATE: *February 21*   COACH: *Coach Pete (signature)*   DATE: *February 21*

Figure 10-2 *(continued)*

effectiveness of their managers and supervisors. This is a harder concept for many managers to accept, probably because they are afraid to face the truth. These are likely the same managers who do not ask their guests for feedback on their dining experiences for fear of hearing something less than complimentary. Since the way you treat your staff is the way they will treat your guests, asking for feedback from them about your performance and finding out how you can be more effective for them will make it easier for them to ask for the same sort of feedback from your guests. Remember that you don't have to be bad to get better. Figure 10-4 suggests a format for a coach/supervisor appraisal. Handle it in a similar manner as suggested above for the Peer Appraisal.

The General Comments section on page 3 provides space for the coach to summarize the person's overall performance and make suggestions for the next appraisal period. The Goals section on page 4 should be developed by the coach and the staff member after they have discussed all the comments on the first three pages. The last section gives the staff member a chance to put his or her own thoughts on the record.

FREQUENCY

Performance appraisal can be a time-consuming (but valuable) process. With the pressures of day-to-day operations, it is also an event that can easily be put off. If you do not conduct regular appraisals, however, it shows that you do not give performance review a high priority and your staff will mirror your attitudes toward appraisal.

To put the company on notice about performance appraisal, we have the following two statements in our Advice to Applicants letter[2] which is given to every prospective staff member:

We expect you to take an active role in your own success and the success of your co-workers. Toward this end, it will be part of your

---

[2]For more information on the Advice to Applicants letter, refer to *The Foolproof Foodservice Selection System.*

Prototype Restaurants
PEER APPRAISAL

Person Being Appraised:	*Never*	*Sometimes*	*Usually*	*Always*
1. CONTRIBUTES TO A POSITIVE ATMOSPHERE: Friendly, cooperates readily with others, flexible, makes things flow more easily, maintains a sense of humor, has a positive outlook, is patient with unexpected change				
2. USES TIME APPROPRIATELY: Reports to work on schedule, respects break time, works efficiently, does not waste time, meets deadlines				
3. DOES THEIR JOB RIGHT: Doesn't miss much, works accurately, follows proper sanitation practices, works safely, meets all company standards, controls waste, gets it right the first time				
4. IS A GOOD TEAM PLAYER: Works well with others, makes co-workers look good, steps in readily when things need to be done, speaks positively about the company and co-workers				
5. CARES ABOUT THEIR WORK: Takes pride in everything they do, maintains high professional standards, conveys a professional image to the public and co-workers				
ADDITIONAL COMMENTS:				

Figure 10-3

Prototype Restaurants
COACH/SUPERVISOR APPRAISAL

Person Being Appraised:	Never	Sometimes	Usually	Always
1. CONTRIBUTES TO A POSITIVE ATMOSPHERE: Friendly, cooperates readily with others, flexible, makes things flow more easily, maintains a sense of humor, has a positive outlook, is patient with unexpected change				
2. SETS A GOOD EXAMPLE: Is a positive role model, holds themselves to the same standards demanded of the staff, speaks positively of the company, guests and staff, does what they say they will do				
3. IS A GOOD TEACHER: Helps me be more effective, answers my questions patiently, listens to my ideas, takes an active interest in my personal and professional development				
4. DEMANDS MY BEST WORK: Consistently upholds company performance standards, is "tough but fair," believes in my ability to improve my performance, challenges me to excel and notices when I do				

Figure 10-4

5. CARES ABOUT THEIR WORK: Takes pride in everything they do, maintains high professional standards, conveys a professional image to the public and staff				
ADDITIONAL COMMENTS:				

Figure 10-4 *(continued)*

job responsibilities to help train your co-workers for positions of higher skill and responsibility. Because of this focus, we will evaluate your performance based not only on your own professional development, but by the advancement of your trainees.

We will regularly evaluate your performance so you know where you stand and how you are doing. The purpose of the appraisals is to assist with your personal and professional development. Much of the responsibility for performance appraisal rests with your coaches, but we will also ask your co-workers to give us their impressions of your work and ask you to do the same of theirs. Their comments will be part of your performance appraisal. We will also ask you to evaluate the effectiveness of your coaches, and that will become part of their performance appraisal. We do not keep secrets from each other or ignore unproductive behavior.

In addition to setting the stage for performance appraisals, making a public statement obligates you to do what you say you will do or risk losing the trust of your staff.

If performance appraisal is just a formal adjunct to consistent one-on-one coaching, it does not need to happen as often to be effective. At the least, you should sit down with everyone once a year to document their progress. You can do it more often, but any more frequently than twice a year is probably overkill.

Part Four
Develop The Team

Chapter Eleven

Share the Power

The fewer facts available, the more people will assume and the more they will be wrong.

—William N. Yeomans

The second most important thing to workers is their desire to be "in" on things. To the extent that your management style regularly includes your staff in the decision-making process, you will create a more positive working climate. To the extent that you cut them out of the loop, you lower the environment on the job.

Today's workers want to be actively involved in their own development. Many of them grew up in an environment where they had a voice and a vote in how things were done. If their parents continually asked for their input at home, what expectations do you think they have when they come to work? The workforce in the 1990s and beyond requires a different work environment to really be effective. The most successful operators in the next decade will be those who most effectively provide a climate where their staff is truly involved in the daily decisions.

Like empowerment, staff involvement will not have a positive impact on the operation if you see it as a technique. People will not get involved if you only try to make them *think* their opinions are important—you must truly see your staff as a vital part of your decision-making process. The shift will come when you start to see them as intelligent, thinking adults who really want to do the best job they can and make a contribution to the success of the organization. It probably was not too long ago that most of us were filling the entry-level positions—and we turned out pretty well! You might as well acknowledge that the people who will be running your operation in the next 5 to 10 years are likely to be clearing tables and washing dishes for you right now.

Human relations consultant Robert Kausen makes these observations about staff involvement:

> *People naturally want to produce excellent results. Contrary to popular misconception, employees really do want to work, and they instinctively want to produce top notch results. When we excel, we feel wonderful. When we throw ourselves into our work, we experience a natural high that inspires us to do even better. High performance feels wonderful and holding back is no fun. It is the total involvement, not the activity, that results in the enjoyment. The enemy of involvement is distraction. You cannot quiet someone's distracted mind, but you can provide a sane climate that promotes healthy mental functioning, thus greater involvement and impact.*

Bringing your crew into the decision-making process is a powerful way to promote a higher climate, improve retention, and increase teamwork. There are two major elements to consider—communication and input.

COMMUNICATION

Someone once said that knowledge is power. The people who will be the building blocks of your success are bright, ambitious, and want to make a contribution. They can only contribute to the extent that they know what is going on in the company. Communication is an easy, yet important first step.

Making sure that everyone stays informed is often a challenge in foodservice. There is seldom a time when everyone is scheduled to be present at one time and staggered reporting times can make even pre-shift meetings tricky. When designing the structure of my own organization, I created a number of communication vehicles in an attempt to overcome these obstacles. Perhaps a quick summary of what I did will give you some ideas you can use to improve the flow of information in your company.

Newsletter

We publish a newsletter every two months (or so) in which we try to cover topics of interest to everyone on the staff, work-related items and announcements, events, and so forth. We invite the crew to let us know when they would like to hear about a particular topic and we do our best to share it with everyone in our newsletter. We encourage them to submit articles or items for the newsletter . . . and are thrilled whenever someone actually does!

Bulletin Boards

We have a bulletin board where we post information for our staff. We invite them to put items of interest on the bulletin board, provided that such items are positive messages and appropriate for our working environment. We try not to censor the material, but I reserve the right to reject tasteless items or negative humor directed at another staff member, the restaurant or the foodservice industry in general, feeling that these detract from a positive working environment.

Trade Publications

We make the principal restaurant trade publications available to our staff. (In most cases, these subscriptions are free.) All coaches and supervisors receive their own copies and are encouraged to share them with their crew. The trade magazines provide good general information about the industry and help everyone catch a glimpse of the bigger picture. We also find that the staff is likely to read these publications closely and often point out great ideas that the managers and supervisors missed. The challenge can easily be one of fielding the many questions and suggestions prompted by their reading. There are worse problems!

Suggestions

We encourage everyone to share their suggestions. We think it is important that we all realize that just because "it has always been done that way," that does not mean it is the only way . . . or even the best way. The key to encouraging people to contribute seems to be for the coaches to resist the urge to make quick judgments about the ideas proposed. Not all staff suggestions are workable as presented, but they often spark other ideas. When we honestly listen to an idea and understood why it makes sense to the person proposing it, we learn a lot about where we can improve. We use the newsletter to acknowledge everyone who offers an idea on how we could do things better, whether or not their recommendation is adopted. Suggestions that result in a cost savings or sales increase typically bring a financial reward as well.

Folders

We mounted some file pockets outside the kitchen office and gave everyone a file folder which serves as their mailbox. We place messages, memos, and other items in the folder. People will only see something if they take it out of their folder, so we encourage everyone to clean out their folder every day to be sure they don't miss anything.

General Meetings

At least once every quarter we hold a meeting for the entire staff to share information and discuss the business. We encourage the crew to participate in these meetings with comments, questions, or suggestions for discussion. Usually, such meetings are to share information of value—"need to know" information for all of us. While there are always items that management wants to present, the best meetings are when we have a true give-and-take about things the staff wants to talk about. Beware of staff meetings that are little more than lectures. When we schedule general meetings, we post a notice on the bulletin board at least two weeks ahead. General meetings are mandatory; we expect everyone to be there and we pay them for their time.

Pre-shift Meetings

Before every shift takes the floor, we *always* take about ten minutes to review items of current importance. These may be events that will happen during the shift (reservations, celebrations, special requests, etc.), recent operating problems, procedure changes, production/service hints, daily goals, and items of general interest to the staff. Staff who miss the pre-shift meeting can find out what they missed by checking the staff briefing book. While there are often pressing events that make it tempting to cancel pre-shift meetings, it is important that they be held no matter what the circumstances of the day. This delivers a clear message to the staff that the pre-shift meetings are very important and creates a more receptive environment for the messages you have to pass on.

Staff Briefing Book

With everyone working different shifts, having days off, and so forth, it is difficult to make sure each person gets "the word" about everything that is going on. To bridge the communication gap, we have a staff briefing notebook where we put important items of information between staff meetings. When a staff member has read something in the book, they simply initial that particular sheet by their name so we know they have seen it. We hold them responsible for everything that is in the book.

We also have two formal ways for the crew to communicate with management:

Hot Line

The Hot Line is a direct link with the Managing Director and is used for questions and work-related comments. The Hot Line is essentially a confidential letter. It is not intended to be a problem resolution tool—we have another very clear process for that. The Managing Director promises to personally answer all such communications within ten days. Blank Hot Line forms are kept by the bulletin boards and can be sent without anyone else's knowledge. Staff members will never suffer any repercussions for submitting a Hot Line.

Committees

The policy-making process in our company is accomplished with the help of a number of committees made up of representatives from all areas of the restaurant and members of the coaching staff. The information that follows explains the committee structure in more detail.

INPUT

The second element of sharing the power, and perhaps the most important, is actually giving your staff a voice in the decisions that influence their lives. This is what workers mean by wanting to be "in" on things. In a team, everyone contributes to the success of the group—that is what makes it a team effort. True teamwork is possible only when every member of the team understands how their actions affect everyone else and that is what the committees help to do.

Particularly when dealing with problems that affect a large number of the staff, I am convinced that the group can arrive at better decisions together than any one person can make alone. The committees do not make the final decisions—that is properly the role of management. However, the committees do advise the coaches and Managing Director in the conduct of the business. I recommend that the committees' input be given serious consideration and only be overruled in extreme cases. If the group's ideas actually form the basis for most operating decisions, the committee process will be validated and accomplish its goal of making the crew part of the process.

For reference, the operation of Prototype Restaurants is enhanced by five committees. Here is a summary of the groups and what they do:

Operations Committee

This committee examines the company's operating systems and proposes solutions to any identified shortcomings. The committee includes the coaches and five staff members representing a cross-section of the restaurant's job functions. This group meets at least once every two weeks.

Rewards and Recognition Committee

This committee selects the All-Star Team each Period and determines how and for what staff members can qualify for Discretionary Fund Bonuses in the coming Period. The Rewards and Recognition Committee also determines to whom Discretionary Fund Bonuses are due for the preceding Period. The membership consists of one coach and five staff members representing a cross-section of the restaurant's job functions. This committee meets at least once every four weeks.

Staff Development Committee

This group advises the coaches and Managing Director on training programs. The Committee studies the effectiveness and relevance of existing programs, recommends additional general programs and may suggest specific improvement plans for individual staff members. The committee includes one coach and five staff members representing a cross-section of the restaurant's job functions. This committee meets at least once every four weeks.

Special Events Committee

This committee coordinates special events and promotions within the restaurant, determines how we will acknowledge seasons and holidays, develops procedures for recognizing guest birthdays, and so forth. The committee consists of one coach and four staff members representing a cross-section of the restaurant. This group meets at lease once every four weeks.

Resolution Comittee

The Managing Director appoints this committee as needed to settle problems between coaches and staff that cannot be resolved through normal procedures. The Committee includes the Human Resources Director, one neutral coach, six neutral staff members, and one member selected by the staff member involved. The Resolution Committee meets as needed.

All restaurant staff members are eligible to serve on committees although they are under no obligation to do so. The Head Coach, Managing Director, or their designee appoints committee members on a rotating basis for a term of three consecutive Periods.

Chapter Twelve

Share the Wealth

In the future, I believe that some form of profit-sharing will be an essential element of commercial foodservice management because it is the best way to get the crew committed to the company's success.
—Michael Brandson, VP, McGuffey's Restaurants

In the past several years, profit-sharing seems to have become a hot topic among owners and managers looking for a way to get their operations in gear. It seems that many operators would like to find a way to implement profit-sharing but they just don't know quite where to start. I suspect there are an infinite number of variations on the theme but let me suggest a simple system that I believe can work for an operation of any size.

EVOLUTION OF A PROFIT-SHARING PLAN

A few years ago, I was contacted by a franchise operator of a national fast food chain. It was a nine-unit organization and the owner was concerned. The recession was deepening, sales were flat, morale was down, the bottom line was eroding, and he was spending all his energy trying to control costs. Being a believer in the power of the group, I felt he would be hard-pressed to turn things around without the help of everyone in the company. Based on my experience, I thought that the most effective way to gain the support of his staff would be to implement a profit-sharing plan.

His immediate reservation about a profit-sharing plan, of course, was that he was barely breaking even and could not figure out how he was going to share profits he did not have. Still, he had no other ideas and decided to see if there was a way to make it work. I met with the district and unit managers (without the owner) for the better part of a day, hammering out a profit-sharing formula that would be fair to all parties and relatively simple to administer.

The first point of agreement was that the owner must cover his monthly obligations before any funds would be distributed. (I had reached agreement on the needed dollar figure before we started the meetings with the managers.) For the sake of the discussion, let's say the owner needed $100,000 per month[1] to cover occupation costs (rent, leases, insurance), provide a return on his investment, and put a few dollars into a reserve fund. We simply agreed to define the bonus fund as that amount of profit in excess of $100,000 per month. Interestingly enough, the major question the managers had was whether $100,000 would be enough! At that point, the owner would have been thrilled to see a bottom line even *close* to that much money every month.

The second step was to determine the distribution formula. After testing all the extremes, the group proposed the following distribution of the operating income in excess of $100,000 every month: 30 percent to the owner, 50 percent to the unit staff and management, and the remaining 20 percent to a fund that the owner and unit managers would mutually administer. This fund would be applied to any purposes decided upon by the group—special bonuses, the purchase of new equipment, and so forth—or held in reserve for future needs.

Since this was a multi-unit operation, there was a secondary split. Of the 50 percent of the profit-sharing pool designated for the restaurants, 50 percent of it was designated for the hourly staff, 30 percent went to the unit management, and 20 percent was retained in a fund in each unit that was jointly administered by the unit staff and management. The discretionary fund was distributed to whomever and for whatever reason the committee decided was in the best interests of the unit.

---

[1]Remember that we are looking at a company with nine operating units.

As we put the finishing touches on the details, the managers were excited. Never before had they been given so much latitude to design a major operating policy. When they presented their plan to the owner, there was a long silence while he considered the proposal. When he declared the split to be "infinitely fair," a profit-sharing plan was born!

What has been the result of implementing the plan? I am not privy to the company's financial results, but I do notice that they are still in business, they have added a new unit, most of the management team is still in place and their units always seem to be busy. For a company that was on the brink of collapse to be in this position after five years in a recessionary economy, I would say that something was working!

So what are the elements of a profit-sharing plan in general (and this approach in particular) that make the idea so effective? Let's look at a few:

Actions Speak Loudly

A profit-sharing plan is a powerful statement about the regard in which you hold your staff, particularly in light of the probability that your competitors are not offering such a plan. The opportunity for your workers to participate in the company's success can make you a more desirable employer and improve the quality of the applicants you attract. Is profit-sharing important to your staff? A good friend of mine tells of hiring an excellent chef away from a competitor—and getting him for a lower salary than he had been making at his previous job—because he was disenchanted with the other operation. Apparently, he had been promised profit-sharing of one-half of one percent of the *net* (probably about $12.00!) and he didn't get it.

Everyone Gets Involved

Profit-sharing is a very team-oriented program because foodservice profits depend on everyone, not just a few stars. In most operations, the guest-contact staff are the ones in the best position to influence sales whereas the production crew typically has more impact on the primary costs. A profit-sharing plan rewards everyone for working together to deliver profits. My friend who stole the chef also reported that she just mentioned to a few people on her staff that she was considering the possibility of implementing a profit-sharing plan. (We are talking about being seriously non-committal here.) She said that she was told more during the next two days about what was happening in her restaurant (waste, poor product, pilferage, etc.) than she had learned from her staff during the previous two years!

The Company Can't Lose

Since the company can decide how much money will be retained before making any split, the owner cannot lose. There is no obligation to share any money until all the bills are paid and there are excess funds available.

The Premise Is Realistic

Profit-sharing is more honest than incentive plans (like dessert contests and the like) because in the real world, you cannot disburse money you do not have. The more the staff understands about how their actions impact on the bottom line, the more effectively they can help the company generate profits.

The Organization Becomes Self-Cleaning

A profit-sharing plan answers the question of "what's in it for me?" Because your crew has a stake in your success, they will tend to straighten out many situations that management cannot easily address. For example, if you suspect a worker of stealing, you have to have all your facts thoroughly documented before you dare make an accusation. However, that person's co-workers do not need documentation—only an indication of misconduct that may affect the profitability of the operation (and the money available for profit-sharing). Peer pressure can frequently put an errant staff member back on track without the need for management involvement.

Equity Is Protected

A profit-sharing plan allows you to reward the staff with a share of the cash flow rather than a share of the ownership. This provides a more immediate return on individual effort and avoids complex bookkeeping when a staff member leaves the company.

Profit-sharing is not all good news, of course. Implementing such a program has a few disadvantages as well:

Bookkeeping

A profit-sharing plan will obviously add some additional accounting requirements to the company's workload. However, since every operation is already calculating income and expense and totalling the number of hours worked by its staff, a program based on hours worked should have minimal impact.

Administration

The amount of administrative time required depends on how you structure the plan. Regardless of the program design, you can expect that not all members of the staff will be eligible to participate in profit-sharing, some will only be qualified to participate for a partial period, and so forth. Keeping track of who is eligible, their basis for participation, payments due and payments made can definitely be time-consuming. The balancing factor is the increased profitability and staff involvement that a profit-sharing plan often brings.

Disclosure

Interestingly, the first objection many owners seem to have about profit-sharing is that it will require them to show their staff the financial statements—and it is true. You will also have to teach your crew how to read the statements and what the numbers mean. I assure you that disclosure has more positive than negative implications.

For a number of years I taught a basic foodservice class for the City of Colorado Springs. Most of the people who attended had some previous foodservice experience. When I got to the section on foodservice economics—where the money comes from and where it goes—I always started by asking the group what percentage of the sales dollar they thought was profit. Invariably, these experienced workers thought that between 25 percent and 50 percent of the dollar represented profit! If you *don't* share the financial results with your staff, they could easily think you are making 50 cents on the dollar! This can be a major issue when they see the amount of their paychecks and recall the sales last Friday night.

Even if you do not choose to implement a profit-sharing plan, I recommend that you regularly review the financial statements with your staff. Unless they know what the business is actually doing and understand how their actions affect the bottom line, they have little ability to know how to build sales, control costs, or conserve resources.

A word of advice: The figure upon which the profit-sharing pool will be based should be operating income[2] since that represents the financial results of the foodservice operation—income and expense over which staff members have some control. Expenses following operating income are really expenses of the real estate aspects of the business (rent, property taxes, insurance, and so forth) over which the staff has no control. Basing the pool on the former figure (i.e., "that amount of money by which operating income exceeds $100,000 per period") allows retention of whatever amount the owner considers necessary to cover occupation costs, return on investment, reserve fund, and so forth, without the need to itemize these items for the staff (unless they ask).

I liked what we had worked out for the fast food company—it was

[2]From "The Uniform System of Accounts for Restaurants," published by the National Restaurant Association. See Figure 12-1.

Summary Statement of Income
Name of Restaurant or Company
Description of Period Covered by Statement

	Amounts	*Percentages*
REVENUE		
Food	$	%
Beverage	————	————
Total Revenue	————	100.00
COST OF SALES		
Food		
Beverage	————	————
Total Cost of Sales	————	————
Gross Profit		
Other Income	————	————
Total Income	————	————
Controllable Expenses		
Salaries and Wages		
Employee Benefits		
Direct Operating Expenses		
Music and Entertainment		
Marketing		
Energy and Utility Services		
Administrative and General Expenses		
Repairs and Maintenance	————	————
Total Controllable Expenses	————	————

Figure 12-1   Uniform System of Accounts for Restaurants
Financial Statement Format

	Amounts	Percentages
OPERATING INCOME		
RENT AND OTHER OCCUPATION COSTS	_____	_____
INCOME BEFORE INTEREST, DEPRECIATION AND INCOME TAXES		
INTEREST	_____	_____
DEPRECIATION	_____	_____
TOTAL	_____	_____
NET INCOME BEFORE INCOME TAXES	_____	_____
INCOME TAXES	_____	_____
NET INCOME	$ _____	_____ %

Figure 12-1 *(continued)*

simple and it made sense. When designing a profit-sharing plan for my own company, I used my experiences with this group as a model, adding what I think are a few interesting twists:

Method of Payment

We set up a 401(k) plan for every member of the regular staff. Instead of being paid directly to the worker, profit-sharing bonuses are paid to this account. In this way, the company is not liable for withholding taxes on the bonus payments and the amounts so disbursed do not increase the wage base for purposes of workers' compensation or unemployment insurance contributions.

Timing

Today's workers are impatient and I wanted them to get their bonuses quickly enough to maintain the connection between the performance and the reward. However, I elected to defer slightly the actual payment of the bonus and use the delay as an incentive for retention. There will be some natural delay due to the time required for accounting and this can be used to your advantage. See Figure 12-2 for details.

Participation

I included all regular staff in the bonus plan since everyone is part of profitability. If everyone's bonus is affected by everyone else's performance, the group will tend to police itself and bring errant workers into the fold (or out in the cold) without the need for management intervention.

Point Bonus

Of the money available for the distribution to the staff, 75 percent was in a point bonus. Participation in the point bonus is based strictly on hours worked, with every regular staff member in good standing earning two points for each hour worked. In addition to points for hours worked, selection to the All-Star Team brings additional points. Because I always hated it when people came in late, the point bonus was structured so that the staff members also lose 5 points per minute for unauthorized absences. The bonus value per point is the amount of money available for the point bonus divided by the total number of points earned during the period.

PROFIT-SHARING BONUS PROGRAM

The company believes those who generate profits should share in those profits. Accordingly, PROTOTYPE RESTAURANTS has set up a profit-sharing bonus program for all regular staff.

ELIGIBILITY

Regular staff members in good standing are eligible to participate in the bonus program. Staff on suspension cannot participate in the bonus program during their suspension. Contingent and temporary staff are not eligible for the bonus program.

BONUS FUND

The bonus fund (the total amount available for bonuses to the staff) is a percentage of Operating Income. This figure may also have a relationship to the dollar amount of Operating Income. PROTOTYPE negotiates the bonus formula with the owner when the company assumes responsibility for operating the restaurant. The Restaurant Supplement explains the bonus fund calculation for your operation.

TYPES OF BONUSES

There are three categories of bonuses:

1. Point Bonus

2. Discretionary Fund Bonus

3. Mr. Clean Bonus

POINT BONUSES

The total amount available for Point Bonuses is 75% of the total bonus fund generated for the Period. Staff earns bonus points on the following basis:

1. Two points for each hour worked.

Figure 12–2   Profit-Sharing Bonus Program
(from the Prototype Staff Manual)

2. Selection to the Period All-Star Team (100, 80, 60, 40 or 20 points).

3. Staff will lose 5 points per minute for unauthorized absences.

The bonus value per point is the amount of money available for the Point Bonus divided by the total number of points earned.

DISCRETIONARY FUND BONUSES

The amount added to the discretionary fund is 25% of the bonus fund generated for the Period. The Rewards and Recognition Committee will determine how, for what and to whom to distribute Discretionary Fund Bonuses each Period.

MR. CLEAN BONUS

Following a regular health department inspection, all members of the staff (regular, contingent and temporary) in good standing could earn a bonus based on the score received by the restaurant. The bonus will be based on the number of hours worked in the complete Periods that have elapsed since the preceding health department inspection. The bonus amount will be as follows:

Score below 85 points	No bonus
Score between 86 and 90	$0.03 per hour worked
Score between 91 and 95	$0.08 per hour worked
Score over 96	$0.15 per hour worked

The Mr. Clean Bonus is not payable for a re-inspection required by a previous low score. The Managing Director will set aside funds from the Discretionary Fund that can only be used for payment of this bonus.

PAYMENT OF BONUSES

The company will pay all bonuses into the staff member's tax-sheltered savings account [401(k) account] 30 days after the end of the Period in which the bonus was earned. For example, Period 1 point bonuses would be paid at the beginning of Period 3.

Figure 12-2 *(continued)*

BONUS PAYMENTS UPON SEPARATION

When a staff member resigns from the company, eligibility for bonus payments is as follows:

1. If the departing individual provides at least four weeks written notice, the company will pay 100% of all point bonuses earned up to the date of departure.

2. If the departing individual provides at least two weeks written notice, but less than four weeks notice, the company will pay all point bonuses earned through the end of the Period preceding the Period of departure. For example, if the staff member gives two weeks notice and leaves sometime during Period 2, the company will pay all point bonuses earned in Period 1.

3. If the departing individual provides less than two weeks notice or is discharged, they are not eligible to receive any unpaid bonuses.

Figure 12-2 *(continued)*

Discretionary Fund Bonus

The balance of the profit-sharing pool went into the Discretionary Fund to be distributed by the Rewards and Recognition Committee.

Mr. Clean Bonus

I am a passionate believer in sanitation. My feeling is that if an operation consistently achieves exceptional scores on its health department inspections, there are a number of other good things that will also be happening. To reinforce this awareness in my staff, the bonus system included a reward—the "Mr. Clean Bonus"—based on our inspection scores. The bonus is based on the score we receive and the number of hours each person has worked since the last inspection. The bonus is structured to provide a real incentive for the team to achieve high scores (and provide real peer pressure for individuals to avoid major mistakes). See Figure 12-2 to see how this bonus was structured.

Bonuses are posted to the worker's 401(k) account 30 days after the end of the period in which the bonus is earned and are not the property of the staff member until they are posted. Having some of the "staff's money" in hand allows the timing and conditions of its transfer to be an incentive for the behavior I want to encourage. I mentioned how the point bonus was structured to encourage workers to report on time. In a similar way, payment of the bonuses was structured to encourage workers to provide adequate notice of their intent to leave the company.

For example, if the departing individual provides at least four weeks' written notice, the company will pay 100 percent of all point bonuses earned right up to the day of departure. If the departing individual provides at least two weeks' written notice, but less than four weeks' notice, the worker will receive all point bonuses earned through the end of the Period preceding the Period of departure. If departing individuals provide less than two weeks' notice or are discharged, they are not eligible to receive any unposted bonuses. The full policy is spelled out in Figure 12-2.

Chapter Thirteen

Other Team-Building Tips

The success of any group of human beings really depends on how
well they can work together.
                              —Herb Kelleher, CEO, Southwest Airlines

There are many ways to help build a team. Without attempting to
provide an exhaustive dissertation on team-building, this chapter
offers some suggestions that will help develop the group feeling that
leads to higher retention, improved morale, and enhanced guest service. Of course, winning teams have been built without any of the
items on this list. These are just some ideas that can help stack the
odds in your favor.

Uniforms

Winning teams have a winning look and that means attractive uniforms that your staff is proud to wear. Some companies have even
gone so far as to allow a staff committee to completely design the
uniforms. Whether uniforms are designed or selected from a cata-
log, people who dress the part tend to act the part. When they look
like a team it helps them act like one.

    If you want everyone to feel like part of the team, everyone on the
staff must have an appropriate uniform, including the production
staff in the kitchen. I found that my cooks particularly appreciated

having their own set of whites with their names embroidered on the chest area. If you are concerned that this will raise your uniform costs beyond what your budget can handle, investigate the possibility of buying good used chefs' apparel from a uniform rental company. I found the cost was *exceptionally* reasonable and allowed me to give my kitchen staff a complete set of working whites that would be theirs forever. They took care of the cleaning, which saved me the cost of renting uniforms.

Outside Events

Company picnics, outings and holiday parties are an excellent way for the staff to establish relationships with each other on a human level as well as on a professional level. The business of foodservice is still foodservice, but a good time now and then can't hurt!

Suggestion Rewards

People do what they are rewarded for. If someone on your staff makes a suggestion that results in a major savings, they are properly entitled to public recognition for their contribution and to receive a share of the savings in the form of a bonus. If you just take the savings and don't give anything back, you are likely to create resentment and stifle future suggestions from your staff. In many people's minds, management is heartless and makes obscene profits from the work of exploited workers. Don't give that stereotype credibility by being greedy or by taking credit for other people's ideas.

Business Cards

When I opened my first restaurant in the mid 1970s, one of my most successful decisions was to have business cards printed for everyone on my staff. This simple, inexpensive gesture probably did more to foster good will and identification with the restaurant than anything else I did.

What I found was that I suddenly had fifty people handing out business cards and extending personal invitations to dine at the restaurant. If the staff member signed their name on the card, it could be redeemed for a complimentary glass of wine or a dessert. The staff did not take advantage of the privilege and genuinely appreciated the trust placed in them. I had a motivated crew who was enthusiastically drumming up both sales volume and good will for the restaurant. Talk about an effective marketing campaign!

The team-building power of the cards is really quite simple—business cards are the mark of a professional in our society. I suspect that most managers would feel that they were not being taken seriously if they did not have business cards. Why would it be any different for the staff?

Depending on the complexity and colors of your artwork, 500 business cards will probably cost you under ten dollars a person to print. In a typical full-service restaurant with about fifty full- and part-time worker, business cards would represent an investment of less than five hundred dollars. How much did your last advertising campaign set you back?

Engraved Nametags

Many operations use nametags for their service staff, but when the worker's name is on just a strip of embossed tape, you run the risk of delivering a message you may not be proud of. The phrase, "What am I, chopped liver?" comes to mind. While I totally understand the thinking behind making nametags easy and inexpensive to make on site, it may be an exercise in false economy. Investing in an attractive, engraved nametag tells your staff that you are proud of them and expect them to stay with you for a while. Who knows? They might just do it! While we are on the subject, be sure to replace plastic nametags when they start to get worn around the edges. It presents a professional image to your guests and reaffirms your commitment to the success of your staff.

In the kitchen, you can pick up points by having the cooks' names embroidered on their chef coats. In my experience, most cooks are delighted to have their own personalized uniforms (just like the serious chefs) and take more pride in their work.

Lockers

Actions speak volumes about the regard in which you hold your workers. It is important that you find space for staff lockers, preferably attractive staff lockers. When they don't have secure lockers, where do people put their valuables? (The answer, of course, is in any nook or cranny that they feel is reasonably safe, regardless of where it is.) This is likely to create a health department violation and make cleaning more difficult. It also makes your staff feel like second-class citizens.

For reasons similar to those outlined regarding nametags, I recommend that you invest in engraved locker nameplates. Space is at a premium in most restaurants, but perhaps there is space along a hallway where you could install lockers. In many operations, some storeroom space can often be reclaimed by increasing the frequency of deliveries and carrying less inventory.

Birthday Cards

Birthdays are special to all of us. A card from the company on a staff member's birthday is a nice gesture. More important, it is a simple acknowledgment that the company recognizes the person on a human level, not just as an employee.

Company Sports Teams

Getting together for non-business activities helps your staff relate to each other as people rather than through the structure created by their business relationships. In most parts of the country there is an active sports program (soccer, basketball, softball, and so forth) offered through a branch of local government. In Colorado Springs, for example, the Parks and Recreation Department offered a number of leagues at different skill levels. If there is interest on the part of your staff, the cost of sponsoring a team is minimal and the benefits can be exceptional.

Tuition Assistance

Think of tuition assistance as your way of sponsoring off-premises training. The advantage of this kind of off-premises training is that you don't have to pay your staff while they are in training. You don't even have to reimburse tuition until *after* the training has been completed. A tuition assistance program can be structured any way you want. Typically, someone has to be on your staff for a specified period of time to be eligible, and reimbursement is based on the grade received. You can also decide which courses or types of courses qualify for support.

Offering tuition assistance can make you a more desirable employer for those workers whose priorities include finishing their education. For an example of a tuition assistance policy, see Figure 13.1.

Staff Discounts

Everybody appreciates a deal. Most operations offer a discount to frequent diners to help build their loyalty. Why not provide an equal (or better) break to your staff? Since most of our workers are always short of cash, a discount allows them to enjoy the experience of dining out in your restaurant. This builds sales, increases their loyalty to the operation, and helps them understand what it is like to be a guest in the restaurant—a perspective that can only help.

On-site Day Care

This may not be a practical option for most restaurants, but it is becoming increasingly more common in hotels. While you may not be able to tackle this on your own, you may be able to take the lead and help organize other businesses in your area (many of whom face the same issues) to set up a day care program that can be offered at a reasonable fee. If you can provide a reasonable answer to the need for day care, you will be a far more attractive employer for working parents.

TUITION SUPPORT PROGRAM

EFFECTIVE DATE:

PROTOTYPE RESTAURANTS recognizes the benefits derived from increased knowledge by our staff. The company will provide tuition support to all staff interested in furthering their formal education.

The Tuition Support Program is a reimbursement program which begins with proof of satisfactory completion of approved course work. Funds for this purpose are separate from those set aside for Training and Development as determined by the company or any restaurant.

Completion of a course of study provides an improved educational background. However, the company will not necessarily reward such accomplishment through promotion, transfer, reassignment or salary increase.

ADMINISTRATIVE RESPONSIBILITY

The HRD will coordinate the Tuition Support Program.

ELIGIBILITY

All regular staff are eligible to apply for tuition support after completing two thousand hours of continuous employment. Rehired former staff will not receive service credit for their previous service. Eligibility will begin following completion of two thousand hours of employment from their new hire date.

APPLICATION

To apply for Tuition Support, staff should complete an Application for Support form and submit it to their coach for review and approval. The coach will forward the form to the HRD for final review and coordination. The staff member will receive a copy of the approved Application for Tuition Support. The HRD will tell the individual if their application is declined.

Figure 13-1   Tuition Support Program
(from the Prototype Restaurants Human Resources Manual)

ELIGIBLE COURSE WORK

The company will only consider tuition support for courses directly related to the staff member's current job. If the nature of the course work is questionable, the individual must provide a summary of the course content. In some cases, the HRD will contact the school directly for further information. Often the title of a particular course does not revel the real nature of the course.

ELIGIBLE EDUCATIONAL INSTITUTIONS

Accredited colleges or universities providing degree programs and technical, trade schools or colleges providing certification are acceptable under this program. The company will not consider correspondence schools or mail order degrees.

FEES COVERED

The Tuition Support Program will reimburse tuition, required text books and required laboratory fees. Tuition Support will not include registration fees, application fees, supplies or equipment. It will not pay for parking fees, transportation fees, room and board fees or other fees.

FINAL GRADE

The company will provide tuition support based on final grade. Because job-related course work benefits both the individual and the company, reimbursement will not exceed 50% of expenses as stated under Fees Covered.

Final Grade of A	50% reimbursement
Final Grade of B	30% reimbursement
Final Grade of C	15% reimbursement
Final Grade D or below	No reimbursement

If the staff member does not submit either required receipts or proof of final grade, the company will not repay expenses. Expenses covered under this policy will not be repaid if any other education assistance program will pay the same expenses.

Figure 13-1 *(continued)*

APPLICATION FOR REIMBURSEMENT

Only those who have received approval for Tuition Support may apply for reimbursement of educational expenses. Staff should complete an Application for Reimbursement and submit original receipts and final grade report. The HRD will return original receipts and grade report after processing the Request for Reimbursement.

METHOD OF REIMBURSEMENT

The company will provide tuition support by making payments to the individual's TSS. Repayment will equal five per cent of the approved tuition support each Period. The company will not advance or pay tuition support in any other manner.

SEPARATION

Upon leaving the company, tuition support will stop and the departing staff member will lose all unpaid tuition support.

TAX CONSIDERATIONS

There may be tax implications to persons receiving tuition support. Staff members are responsible for such taxes, if any, and must seek counsel from a tax professional.

Figure 13-1 *(continued)*

Professional Library

If you seek out and encourage professional curiosity in your staff, you are unlikely to ever be able to offer all the personal and professional development your staff will want. To satisfy this demand, you can start to build a professional library for the use of your management and staff. Over the years, you can accumulate an impressive collection of educational material (audio tapes, video tapes, books, and so forth) that your crew can check out for study on their own. The better they become, the better the company will become—and it happens on their own time.

To gain the most from your library, budget funds every year for library acquisitions and solicit suggestions from your staff about what material to add. They will get more involved in the company and you are more likely to have the library utilized.

Company Rituals

Rituals and ceremonies help establish and preserve the company's culture. Such events as the passage from contingent to regular staff, employment anniversaries, and job promotions all warrant something more visible (and meaningful) than just a quiet entry in the personnel record. Having these important events acknowledged in the presence of one's peers makes them more special and provides a greater feeling of accomplishment.

A very effective enhancement of these rituals is to accompany the ceremony with a visible symbol, such as a small pin or different color nametag. Many special occasions might be accompanied by new business cards. All these factors make it easier for workers to feel that they are a part of the operation, provide them with a sense of motion, and support their pride in personal and professional accomplishments.

Team Photos

Every sports team takes a team picture every year. Why should a foodservice operation be any different? There is always the problem of one or two people being unavailable and the general difficulty of getting everyone together at the same time, but a great color shot of the whole gang every year can be a real morale-builder and source of identity with the group.

Fun

Remember that people go to restaurants for a good time as well as a good meal. To be sure the guests have fun, it is important that the staff enjoy themselves as well. Earlier we discussed the idea that people are more productive in a higher state of mind. Allow people to have fun and it will help keep things loose. When the pressure is off, most workers will easily slip into a better mood because people's natural state of mind is high.

Managers should make it a point not to lose their sense of humor. Smiles also have a positive effect. If you start to feel stressed-out or begin to take yourself too seriously, put on a pair of "Groucho glasses"—the horned-rim specials with the nose and moustache attached—and wear them around the dining room for a few minutes. That will help loosen you up!

As a final suggestion, do something outrageous every once in a while. You could wash every staff member's car while they are working, give someone a few paid hours off and take their shift, hand out lottery or concert tickets or cook breakfast for the morning shift. Let your imagination and sense of silliness guide you. The goal is to regularly share a laugh with your staff and give them stories to tell others. After all, isn't that the way you want them to treat your guests? Build fun and lightness into your company in any way you can. Foodservice can be a stressful business and we must actively try to keep that feeling of stress from reaching our staff members or our guests.

There are no limits to what you can do to help your staff identify more closely with your operation and with each other. This is certainly not an exhaustive list of the ways to build a foodservice team. Still, it should provide a few ideas that can help you get started. The more your crew pulls together and the more they trust your motives, the more suggestions they will offer on how you can strengthen the team.

Part Five
Take the Temperature

Chapter Fourteen

Evaluate Your Retention Climate

Basically, the business of business is people.
—Herb Kelleher, CEO, Southwest Airlines

The same working climate that causes your staff to want to stay will also make your guests want to return more often. Care and feeding of the climate involves addressing a number of questions, the answers to which will help you understand what is happening in your organization.

To assess the retention climate in your operation, answer the following questions honestly. Avoid wishful thinking. If you want a more precise picture, ask your staff members to complete this quiz (anonymously, of course).

EVALUATE YOUR RETENTION CLIMATE

For each question, mark "Yes (Y)" if the statement is always true, "No (N)" if the answer is not indicative of your operation and "Maybe or Not Sure (?)" if your results in this area are ambiguous or inconsistent.

Y	N	?	
❑	❑	❑	1. *Are* you the best employer in town?
❑	❑	❑	2. Does your operation have a reputation for professional excellence?
❑	❑	❑	3. Are your wages at or above prevailing rates in your area?
❑	❑	❑	4. Have you created meaningful jobs?
❑	❑	❑	5. Do you see labor hours as an investment in building sales and guest gratification?
❑	❑	❑	6. Does your crew participate in the decisions that affect their careers?
❑	❑	❑	7. Do you treat your staff the same way you treat your guests?
❑	❑	❑	8. Do you measure your personal success by the success of your staff?
❑	❑	❑	9. Are you more of a coach than a cop?
❑	❑	❑	10. Do you keep statistics on staff retention?
❑	❑	❑	11. Is the retention rate part of the performance appraisal for your coaching staff?
❑	❑	❑	12. Are the performance appraisals of your staff based on results instead of activities?
❑	❑	❑	13. Do you provide a benefit program for coaching staff?
❑	❑	❑	14. Do you provide a benefit program for full-time workers?
❑	❑	❑	15. Do you provide a benefit program for part-time workers?
❑	❑	❑	16. Do you require that you and your staff take paid vacations at least once a year?
❑	❑	❑	17. Do you reward staff members for going beyond the norm to delight guests?
❑	❑	❑	18. Do you consistently reinforce your crew's feeling of self-worth?
❑	❑	❑	19. Do you consistently and effectively convey your gratitude to your staff for their work?
❑	❑	❑	20. Do you place more value on avoiding problems than on solving problems?

Y	N	?	
❏	❏	❏	21. Do you have a written staff manual or hand-book?
❏	❏	❏	22. Do you have written human resources policies?
❏	❏	❏	23. Is your operations manual limited to no more than ten key points?
❏	❏	❏	24. Is your procedures manual minimal?
❏	❏	❏	25. Do you conduct regular performance appraisals?
❏	❏	❏	26. Do you provide uniforms that your staff is proud to wear?
❏	❏	❏	27. Do you insist on hearing "bad news" quickly?
❏	❏	❏	28. Do you treat all your staff equally?
❏	❏	❏	29. Do you see behavior as a symptom instead of as the problem?
❏	❏	❏	30. Do you take a benefit-of-the-doubt stance toward your staff?
❏	❏	❏	31. Do you and your coaching staff have a satisfying life *outside* the operation?
❏	❏	❏	32. Does everyone in your employ know that you have a sense of humor?
❏	❏	❏	33. Do you have a profit-sharing or bonus plan based on profitability?
❏	❏	❏	34. Do you know the personal and professional goals of each member of your staff?
❏	❏	❏	35. Are you actively helping them achieve these goals?
❏	❏	❏	36. Do you praise your staff members at least twice as often as you criticize them?
❏	❏	❏	37. Do you know the names of everyone on your staff?
❏	❏	❏	38. Do you conduct a formal orientation program for all new staff members?
❏	❏	❏	39. Do you encourage your staff to experiment and try new ideas?
❏	❏	❏	40. Do you support your staff if they fail?
❏	❏	❏	41. Does your crew always know how well they are meeting your expectations?

Y	N	?	
❑	❑	❑	42. Do you have a regular, effective means of communication within the company?
❑	❑	❑	43. Do you have an active, ongoing training program for all staff levels?
❑	❑	❑	44. Do you have periodic company gatherings strictly for the fun of it?
❑	❑	❑	45. Do you truly expect the best from each member of your staff?
❑	❑	❑	46. Do you encourage (and financially support) attendance at professional seminars?
❑	❑	❑	47. Do you prohibit yourself and your coaching staff from working over 45 hours a week?
❑	❑	❑	48. Do you always play as good a game as you talk?
❑	❑	❑	49. Do you go out of your way to accommodate special requests from your staff?
❑	❑	❑	50. Are you having fun yet?

Score the test by awarding yourself two points for a "Yes," one point for a "Maybe," and no points for a "No." Here is an idea of what your score means:

90–100	Give yourself an A! You are a super climate-builder and your success is no accident.
80–89	Excellent. You are well on your way to becoming the best employer in town.
70–79	Very good. Your heart is in the right place. Keep working on it.
60–69	Good . . . and you know you can do better. The rewards are worth it.
50–59	Okay . . . and you need to make some adjustments to stay ahead of the competition.
Below 50	Time to take a serious look at your business and make that self-improvement action plan.

Source: Bill Marvin, *The Foolproof Foodservice Selection System*, excerpted with permission.

Implementing the ideas in this book and its predecessor, *The Fool-proof Foodservice Selection System*, can be an effective way to start improving your retention rate and enhancing your team spirit.

As a second step, consider the points raised in the quiz questions and see what you can do to improve your score. Any modifications you can make that will enhance your general working environment will improve your retention climate, make your work easier, and keep your staff happier. It is all money in your pocket. You just have to want to do it and be willing to start somewhere. It is never too late to become a legend!

Glossary

To illustrate how many of the ideas in this book might be applied, I have provided excerpts from the manuals I developed for my restaurant management company, Prototype Restaurants. This glossary explains terms and abbreviations in the manuals. Here are the terms and what they mean:

Coach Head Coach and Assistant Coaches—in other companies they would be called managers

Company PROTOTYPE RESTAURANTS

Confirmation Period the trial or adjustment period for new staff

Contingent Staff newly hired staff during their confirmation period

Discharge involuntary separation from the company

Dismissal involuntary separation from the company

Guest customers of the restaurants (we don't use the word *customer* in the company)

HRD Human Resources Director—the person in the company responsible for personnel matters

Managing Director the person responsible for the overall operation of PROTOTYPE RESTAURANTS

Period a regular 4-week accounting period—used instead of months

Regular Staff staff who have successfully completed their confirmation period

Resignation voluntary separation from the company

Restaurant any restaurant operated by the company

Restaurant Supplement the guidebook for each particular restaurant

Staff employees of PROTOTYPE RESTAURANTS (we don't use the word *employee* in the company)

Temporary Staff people hired for a specific period of time, usually less than 120 days

TSS tax-sheltered savings account (technically known as a 401(k) plan)

Resources for Retention

BOOKS

De Pree, Max, *Leadership is an Art*, 1989, Dell Publishing, 666 Fifth Avenue, New York, NY 10103.

Drummond, Karen Eich, *The Restaurant Training Program*, John Wiley & Sons, Inc., 605 Third Avenue, New York, NY 10158.

Kausen, Robert, *Customer Satisfaction Guaranteed*, 1988, Life Education, Inc., St. Rt. 2-3969, Trinity Center, CA 96091.

LeBoeuf, Michael, *The Greatest Management Principle in the World*, Berkley Publishing Group, 200 Madison Avenue, New York, NY 10016.

Marvin, Bill, *The Foolproof Foodservice Selection System: The Complete Manual for Creating a Quality Staff*, 1993, John Wiley & Sons, Inc., 605 Third Avenue, New York, NY 10158.

Marvin, Bill, *Restaurant Basics: Why Guests Don't Come Back and What You Can Do About It*, 1992, John Wiley & Sons, Inc., 605 Third Avenue, New York, NY 10158.

National Restaurant Association, *The First Day*, Educational Foundation of the National Restaurant Association, 250 South Wacker Drive, Chicago, IL 60606.

Pryor, Karen, *Don't Shoot the Dog! The New Art of Teaching and Training*, 1984, Bantam Books, 666 Fifth Avenue, New York, NY 10103.

Townsend, Robert, *Further Up the Organization*, Harper & Row, 10 East 53rd Street, New York, NY 10022.

Yeomans, William N., *1000 Things You Never Learned in Business School*, 1985, Mentor Books, 1633 Broadway, New York, NY 10019.

AUDIO TAPES

Kausen, Robert, Life Education, Inc., St. Rt. 2-3969, Trinity Center, CA 96091, (916) 266-3235.

Prototype Restaurants, PO Box 280, Gig Harbor, WA 98335, (800) 767-1055.

VIDEO TAPES

Kausen, Robert, Life Education, Inc., St. Rt. 2-3969, Trinity Center, CA 96091, (916) 266-3235.

Educational Foundation of the National Restaurant Association, 250 South Wacker Drive, Suite 1400, Chicago, IL 60606, (800) 765-2122.

Prototype Restaurants, PO Box 280, Gig Harbor, WA 98335, (800) 767-1055.

SOURCES FOR MANUALS

Prototype Restaurants, PO Box 280, Gig Harbor, WA 98335, (800) 767-1055.

Bill Main & Associates, 2560 North Avenue, Chico, CA 95926, (800) 858-7876.

EXIT INTERVIEWS

Hospitality Service Group, PO Box 280, Gig Harbor, WA 98335, (800) 767-1055.

ORGANIZATIONS

Council of Hotel and Restaurant Trainers, 1144 Wildwood Lane, Bluffton, IN 46714, (219) 824-8932.

International Foodservice Executives Association, 110 South State Road 7, Margate, FL 33068, (800) 544-3732.

National Restaurant Association, 1200 Seventeenth Street, NW, Washington, DC 20036, (800) 424-5156.

About the Author

William R. Marvin, "The Restaurant Doctor™," is an advisor to restaurateurs across the country. Bill is the founder of PROTOTYPE RESTAURANTS, a restaurant consulting, development and management company based in the Pacific Northwest.

Bill is a member of the Council of Hotel and Restaurant Trainers (CHART). He is one of the first to earn certification as a Foodservice Management Professional from the National Restaurant Association and has been designated as a Certified Foodservice Executive by the International Foodservice Executives Association. He was a Director of the Colorado Restaurant Association for seven years and taught a continuing vocational foodservice class for the City of Colorado Springs, Colorado.

He started in the industry at the age of fourteen, washing dishes in a small restaurant on Cape Cod. He went on to earn a degree in Hotel Administration from Cornell University. Bill moved to Colorado in 1984 to design the foodservice system for the U.S. Olympic Training Centers and relocated to the Puget Sound area of Washington State in 1993.

Before joining the Olympic Committee, Bill spent twelve years in San Francisco. He was a supervisor in the management consulting department of Laventhol & Horwath, a national hospitality consulting firm. He developed and operated two restaurants of his own. He was also an independent restaurant consultant specializing in marketing, new concept development, and Chapter 11 reorganizations.

His hands-on operational experience includes hotels, clubs, restaurants, and institutions. He has managed a condominium hotel in the Caribbean and a prestigious New England country club, and has worked as a consultant/designer for a national food facilities engineering firm. He has also operated several enlisted feeding facilities as an officer in the U.S. Navy, the largest serving over 20,000 meals a day. This wide range of experience has contributed to his broad perspective on the industry and enabled him to be effective in all types and sizes of foodservice operations.

He is the author of the acclaimed books *Restaurant Basics: Why Guests Don't Come Back and What You Can Do About It* and *The Foolproof Foodservice Selection System: The Complete Manual for Creating a Quality Staff*, both published by John Wiley & Sons. He has also published a pocket guide to service entitled *50 Tips to Improve Your Tips*. Bill is a frequent contributor to national industry trade magazines. In addition to his private consulting practice, he conducts management training seminars across North America.

You can contract Bill at PROTOTYPE RESTAURANTS, PO Box 280, Gig Harbor, WA 98335. His toll-free telephone number is (800) 767-1055.

Index

COACHING REPORT

NAME:		PERIOD COVERED:		REPORT PREPARED BY:

ACTIVITIES	RESULTS DESIRED	RESULTS OBSERVED	COMMENTS

COACHING REPORT

EVALUATION FACTORS	RESULTS DESIRED	RESULTS OBSERVED	COMMENTS

COACHING REPORT

Peer Appraisal

EVALUATION FACTORS	NEVER	SOMETIMES	USUALLY	ALWAYS	GENERAL PEER COMMENTS
Contributes to a positive atmosphere					
Uses time appropriately					
Does their job right					
Is a good team player					
Cares about their work					

General Comments and Suggestions from the Coaches

COACHING REPORT

Goals for Next Appraisal Period

Staff Member's Comments

My coach and I have discussed my performance including all the comments and suggestions above. I understand the reasoning behind all comments included in this report.

STAFF MEMBER: _____ DATE: _____ COACH: _____ DATE: _____

PEER APPRAISAL

PERSON BEING APPRAISED:	NEVER	SOMETIMES	USUALLY	ALWAYS
1. CONTRIBUTES TO A POSITIVE ATMOSPHERE: Friendly, cooperates readily with others, flexible, makes things flow more easily, maintains a sense of humor, has a positive outlook, is patient with unexpected change				
2. USES TIME APPROPRIATELY: Reports to work on schedule, respects break time, works efficiently, does not waste time, meets deadlines				
3. DOES THEIR JOB RIGHT: Doesn't miss much, works accurately, follows proper sanitation practices, works safely, meets all company standards, controls waste, gets it right the first time				
4. IS A GOOD TEAM PLAYER: Works well with others, makes co-workers look good, steps in readily when things need to be done, speaks positively about the company and co-workers				
5. CARES ABOUT THEIR WORK: Takes pride in everything they do, maintains high professional standards, conveys a professional image to the public and co-workers				
ADDITIONAL COMMENTS:				

COACH/SUPERVISOR APPRAISAL

PERSON BEING APPRAISED:	NEVER	SOMETIMES	USUALLY	ALWAYS
1. CONTRIBUTES TO A POSITIVE ATMOSPHERE: Friendly, cooperates readily with others, flexible, makes things flow more easily, maintains a sense of humor, has a positive outlook, is patient with unexpected change				
2. SETS A GOOD EXAMPLE: Is a positive role model, holds themselves to the same standards demanded of the staff, speaks positively of the company, guests and staff, does what they say they will do				
3. IS A GOOD TEACHER: Helps me be more effective, answers my questions patiently, listens to my ideas, takes an active interest in my personal and professional development				
4. DEMANDS MY BEST WORK: Consistently upholds company performance standards, is "tough but fair," believes in my ability to improve my performance, challenges me to excel and notices when I do				
5. CARES ABOUT THEIR WORK: Takes pride in everything they do, maintains high professional standards, conveys a professional image to the public and staff				
ADDITIONAL COMMENTS: